Supporting Birth Parents Whose Children Have Been Adopted

Supporting Birth Parents Whose Children Have Been Adopted

Edited by Joanne Alper

Forewords by Dr John Simmonds OBE
and The Rt Hon Sir Andrew McFarlane

Jessica Kingsley *Publishers*
London and Philadelphia

First published in 2019
by Jessica Kingsley Publishers
73 Collier Street
London N1 9BE, UK
and
400 Market Street, Suite 400
Philadelphia, PA 19106, USA

www.jkp.com

Library of Congress Cataloging in Publication Data
A CIP catalog record for this book is available from the Library of Congress

British Library Cataloguing in Publication Data
A CIP catalogue record for this book is available from the British Library

ISBN 978 1 78592 323 4
eISBN 978 1 78450 638 4

Printed and bound by CPI Group (UK) Ltd, Croydon, CR0 4YY

*To all birth parents brave enough to face their past
so they can work towards a more hopeful future.*

Contents

Part I: Evaluation of Therapeutic Support for Birth Parents (Hertfordshire University)

Part II: A Trauma-Informed and Relationship-Based Approach to Therapeutic Support for Birth Parents (Adoptionplus)

Part III: A Group Work Model (After Adoption)

Part IV: Creating Space for Change: Supporting Women Who Have Experienced Recurrent Care Proceedings (Pause)

Foreword

Dr John Simmonds OBE

The history of adoption has always been strongly influenced by a 'rescue perspective' – babies or very young children who needed to be rescued from their mothers who had become pregnant outside of marriage and in that sense giving birth to an illegitimate child. And over the last 50 years, rescued from abusive and neglectful mothers. Fathers have played a minimal part in much of this narrative. Adoptive parents have had a more prominent and positive role and to some degree that of the children. This position continues to reflect much that drives current policy and practice. And there are deeply troubling themes emerging such as the large numbers of women who have repeat pregnancies only for those children to be removed. The characteristics of these women – their young age, learning difficulties, drug and alcohol problems, serious mental health problems and experience of domestic violence are very familiar. Fathers continue to be largely invisible even where they have very similar profiles. Both the birth mothers and fathers are among the most vulnerable, most oppressed and most excluded individuals in society.

This collection of chapters is a serious and not to be missed challenge to current policy and practice. They re-assert the opportunity that the crisis of a child being removed and placed for adoption brings despite the loss, grief, anger, despair and trauma that accompany this both in the present and long into their futures. And they offer informed, deliverable and positive interventions where this opportunity might become a turning point in the lives of the birth parents. There is no suggestion about this being simple or straightforward – any trust is likely to have seriously broken down in the birth parents when offers of help are made, the range of issues faced by the parents can be overwhelming, and a long-term perspective with sufficient resources a priority.

Alper has brought together a wide range of informed experiences and practice opportunities that address all of these issues. The overall perspective is sensitive, empathetic, realistic, hopeful and robust. And it should inform the development of a strategic and operational framework into the future that is as central as many of the developments that have come to inform services to adoptive parents and adopted children. If there are lessons to be learnt from almost 100 years of adoption policy and practice, it is that birth parents must be included in every stage of the process without that being framed in a simplistic, blaming way and as just one more demand on our time and resources. Alper and colleagues reminds us of this in every word, sentence and chapter.

Dr John Simmonds OBE
Director of Policy, Research and Development
CoramBAAF

Foreword

The Rt Hon Sir Andrew McFarlane

In the aftermath of contested court proceedings which have resulted in the adoption of a child it is, I suspect, all too easy for the social work professionals, lawyers and judges involved to move on to the next case and, if thought is given at all to the human beings who have been through the court process, the focus will be on the positive outcome for the child and their future in a new, adoptive, family. Joanne Alper and her colleagues are to be congratulated for producing this important book which does much to recalibrate the zoom of the reader's lens to take in the birth parents, who leave the court having lost the proceedings and facing the future with a massive hole in the centre of their lives.

This book is important for a number of reasons. Firstly, whilst there has been some work and reference in the professional literature to birth parents after adoption, that material has not, until now, been drawn together and presented as a whole in the manner that is achieved in Chapter 1.

Secondly, the book highlights the benefits of working with post-adoption birth parents. These benefits are clearly identifiable where the parent may well go on to have further children; but there are, as is well demonstrated here, benefits in supporting parents who may have some contact with the adopted child in the years to come. The need for this support applies equally, whether the contact is planned or may take place clandestinely or haphazardly via social media or, simply through the adult child finding their birth family in adulthood. In any event, parents post-adoption, who by definition are vulnerable and must be damaged by the process, are likely to be in need of counselling and support simply for their own emotional health and mental wellbeing.

Thirdly, throughout the narrative the text is brought alive by direct quotation from parents and counsellors in a manner which demonstrates so clearly the emotions that are in play and the manner in which parents, over time, may be assisted to a more positive space and outlook.

Fourthly, the book highlights the work undertaken by the Adoptionplus Birth Relative Counselling Service and contains a stage-by-stage account of the flexible and client-focussed approach that its counsellors bring to this work. As someone peering in to this world from the outside, I found the diary-style description of 'Carrie's Story' in Chapter 6 particularly illuminating.

Fifthly, as well as giving space to describe the excellent and well known work of 'Pause', readers are introduced to an alternative model, 'Breaking the Cycle', which has been developed by After Adoption, and which does not require parents to commit to contraception.

For these various reasons, I thoroughly commend this book to all those with an interest in Adoption. Joanne Alper, her team of writers, and, above all, the professional team at Adoptionplus whose work is championed here, are to be congratulated in sharing this material with a wider readership in such an accessible format.

The President of the Family Division
The Right Honourable Sir Andrew McFarlane

Acknowledgements

Joanne Alper

This book has been very important to me and I'm so thankful that I have been able to work with such a great team to bring it together. Firstly, I want to thank all the birth parents who have contributed to this book, both directly via their poems and stories, and indirectly via the insights gained from listening to them over the years and hearing their pain and the challenges they face. Many brave and inspiring people who battle on a daily basis to manage and overcome the difficulties that life has presented them with. Please know that we see your courage and we know that you wish circumstances could have been different.

A special thanks goes to 'Carrie', an amazing and courageous birth mother who has allowed us to share the details of her story in the hope that it will help other parents. 'Carrie' you know who you are... Thank you for all of your support with this book and keep battling for your own healthy and more hopeful future!

I'd also like to acknowledge the wonderful and moving input of the Adoptionplus counsellors who have contributed to this book. The respectful and sensitive manner in which you have shared parents' stories alongside your compassion, insight and professional skills, has brought to life the work you do and will encourage the development of improved and more effective practice in this sector. I know it's not been easy going from counsellors to 'paperback writers', but your dedication and perseverance have paid off...super proud of you all!

Thanks also goes to Hertfordshire University, and managers from Pause and After Adoption, whose contributions and commitment to services for birth parents shine through in both the way they work and the way in which they write. The recent closure of After Adoption means that although we have lost their pioneering services, the models they developed leave a legacy for others to build on.

A really big thanks goes to Jo Meyjes whose commitment and support for this book and the messages it aims to convey, has been enormously valued and appreciated. Dedicated, conscientious and passionate about effective services for birth parents, your support runs right through this book. Another really big thanks goes to Ros Brown for all of your help in the completion of this book. Your organisational skills and efficiency are inspiring and almost magical!

I'd also like to thank two amazing Clinical Psychologists, Dr Kim Golding and Dr Karen Treisman, for believing in this book and what it seeks to communicate. Thank you for your knowledge, your insights and your compassion. Your practice and your words continue to shine beacons that light the way for others.

Lastly, I absolutely have to thank my husband and family who have been amazing and have patiently supported me as I sought to find time to write and edit this book. An uber special thanks goes to Evie and Lily for your understanding, your wisdom and your unwavering belief that this book would get finished!

Introduction

Joanne Alper

I have three holes in my heart

No surgeon could repair them

No scan could see them

But I have three holes in my heart.

Adoption today is a child welfare intervention, the aim of which is to provide permanent homes for children who cannot live with parents or relatives. Where thresholds of harm have been clearly established in court, then the child's welfare is prioritised over that of their parents, who, understandably, often will not want their child to be adopted.

The public perception of birth parents who have had their children removed and placed for adoption is varied. Some people vilify them, for having hurt or allowed their children to be hurt and abused. Others see them as the victims of an authoritarian state that has abused its power by interfering in the sanctity of family life and the rights that parents have over their children. These public perceptions can get in the way of really understanding the needs of this group and the best way to support them.

As a society, we don't want our children to be neglected and abused. If the state becomes aware that this is happening, there is a moral duty to intervene and try and protect children from further harm. Clearly the best way to do this is to help and support parents to change their behaviour, so they can safely care for and nurture their children. Legislation and social work training all promote and encourage an approach that focuses on trying to help birth parents improve their parenting. Despite this focus, sometimes the birth parents' own difficulties mean that they are unable to make the changes needed. If, regardless of support provided, parents remain unable to safely care for their children, clearly someone needs to step in to nurture those children as they grow into adulthood. This can be a family member or, if this isn't possible, then adoption will be considered. The focus at this point is on what's best for the child. As young children need stable, caring family lives, without unnecessary state involvement, adoption may be considered for some children as an option that is right for them.

Social workers and courts will be concentrating on the child and their needs, as plans are carefully considered for their future. With compassion and empathy reasonably directed to the children and time and resources limited, it can sometimes be difficult for the childcare social workers to consider the birth parents and their needs. Local Authorities do not have social work teams to support birth parents whose children have been removed and parents are mostly left to manage alone.

The Adoption and Children Act was introduced in 2002 in order to increase birth relatives' rights to support services. This was further strengthened in 2005 and since this time it has been a legal requirement for Local Authorities to provide independent support and counselling for birth parents and other relatives before, during and after adoption. However the quality and quantity of this provision is varied throughout the UK. In addition, birth parents themselves are often reluctant to take up the services that are provided, making the whole situation even more complex. This book aims to provide better understanding of the needs of birth parents in order that services are provided in ways that are both accessible and helpful.

Providing effective counselling support to birth parents can have a multitude of benefits. First, counselling support can be enormously helpful for birth parents in their own right, as human beings in considerable emotional pain. Many are trying to manage a range of difficulties that life has presented them with. If people have a history of abuse and neglect themselves and have never experienced healthy relationships or healthy parenting, it can be difficult for them to understand and meet their own needs let alone the needs of their children. Additionally, we do know from research that actually having your children removed by the state and placed for adoption in itself can result in a deterioration in parents' mental health. So, emotionally fragile people can become even more damaged by the removal of their children. If parents are willing to accept support and want to change how they feel and the direction their life is taking, we would argue that we have a responsibility to do what we can to assist them.

Parents who lose a child to adoption often go on to have further children and those children may also be removed because of harmful parenting. Providing support to birth parents provides an opportunity to potentially stop the cycle; stop further children being hurt and prevent further children coming into the care system. The human benefits are absolutely huge to the adults and children affected. Additionally, at a time when resources are increasingly becoming more scarce for Local Authorities, providing effective support to this high-risk group can clearly be considered as targeted prevention and a sensible way to strategically manage limited resources.

Birth parents whose children have been adopted still have a role in their children's lives, either directly via some form of contact or more indirectly associated with their children's sense of their identity.

Once a child is adopted, contact usually takes the form of yearly letter exchange, managed by the Local Authority. For some it may even involve meeting again once their children reach adulthood, if this is something their children want to do. However, increasingly with the rise of social media it may also involve re-establishing some form of unmanaged contact when their children are still young and vulnerable. In their struggles with identity and in the absence of information, young children can try and find their birth families. The unmanaged and unsupported nature of these situations can often be detrimental to children. However, should contact in adoption be viewed differently and should it be properly and effectively supported, there is the potential that it could in fact be helpful for children in some circumstances. Central to any success is the need to properly support the birth parents, so that they in turn can properly support their children, should the circumstance arise.

This book aims to increase understanding of the needs of birth parents and consider effective approaches for therapeutic support. We will be discussing different models of intervention, from the practical to the more therapeutic and exploring what research and evaluation tell us about what works. Throughout the book we will be hearing directly from birth parents themselves through their poems and prose, as we believe it's essential that their voices are heard. The birth parents who contributed to this book wanted professionals to understand the pain they were in and wanted to ensure practice is improved for other birth parents who find themselves in similar situations.

The hope is that all of this will promote greater understanding of birth parents, of their experiences and of their counselling support needs. Not only to create more compassion for their pain, but also to encourage the development of more effective counselling support services for them nationally. Not all birth parents would want or even recognise a need for support. However, for those who do, we believe that counselling support should be provided. The aim is that by sharing the learning from organisations currently providing services to birth parents, we can assist in the development of more effective services across the United Kingdom.

Adoption in the United Kingdom

Forms of adoption have always existed in the United Kingdom, in the sense of people taking care of other people's children when needed and bringing them up as their own. However, there had been no legal basis for adoption until the 20th century. During this period the Adoption Act 1926 was introduced and since then almost every decade has seen new laws introduced that have increasingly regulated the process. Adoption has changed over the decades since this first legislation and, alongside these changes, so has our knowledge and understanding of the needs of adopted children and adoptive parents. The majority of children who are now adopted in the United Kingdom are mainly from Local Authority Care, where they have been looked after as a result of abuse and neglect experienced within their birth families. In recent years, when considering the needs of the adoptive families there has been increasing recognition of the need for a more therapeutic approach with greater emphasis on openness about adoption itself, support for letter contact with birth relatives and an increased understanding of the adoption support needs of adoptive families. However, there appears to have been only minimal reflection on the support needs of birth parents and, with it, the improved contribution they could potentially make to their children's lives.

It is apparent that adoption has been seen over the decades as a solution to a changing number of social problems. At the centre of all of these is the desire to do what is best for children. However, consistent throughout the decades is the lack of focus on the support needs of birth parents. This book aims to focus on the therapeutic support needs of birth parents whose children have been adopted over recent years. We do not seek to comment on the rights or wrongs of the adoption decision itself, instead we will be focusing on the aftermath for birth parents. Adoption has changed over the years and in our view the way we consider support for birth parents also needs to change.

We recognise that many birth parents often require support with finance, housing, education, employment, health and other more practical issues, however the focus of this particular book is on promoting greater understanding of services needed to support them with their emotional health. We hope this book is viewed as a beginning to further debate, research and understanding on how best to provide therapeutic support for this high-need, but often much-neglected group. The Adoptionplus therapeutic service discussed in the book is in essence based on person centred therapy, with counsellors also trained in Dyadic Developmental Psychotherapy, Eye Movement Desensitisation and Reprocessing (EMDR), Sensorimotor Psychotherapy and MBCT Mindfulness. However, we are aware that there are additionally a number of trauma-specific therapeutic interventions that could also be helpful to birth parents. Our hope is that as services develop in this area, so will understanding as to which therapeutic approaches are the most effective. This book aims to share information about the experiences of birth parents and those currently working therapeutically with them, in the hope of promoting greater understanding and improved service development.

Contributors include Dr Lizette Nolte, Dr Hannah Morgan, Caoimhe Forbes and Dr Hannah Wright from Hertfordshire University Psychology Department; Carole Green, Ian Orr-Campbell, Dr Kim S. Golding, Jane Gould and Patricia Downing from Adoptionplus Birth Relative Counselling Service; Daljit Gill and Bethany Lambert from After Adoption; and Sophie Humphreys and Ellen Marks from Pause. Finally, Dr Karen Treisman will be drawing all the information together in the Conclusion. Importantly, also contributing will be the birth parents themselves through their poems and prose.

Chapter overview
Chapter 1: How Best to Support Birth Relatives:
What the Experts Say
The first chapter considers nationally and internationally what is known about the psychological and emotional needs of birth parents and how

best to support them. Lizette Nolte, Hannah Morgan and Caoimhe Forbes from Hertfordshire University undertake a literature review looking at what is known about counselling and support services that currently exist and whether they are effective. They go on to highlight some important themes that they wish the reader to consider.

The chapter starts by discussing the psychological and emotional needs of birth parents. Nolte *et al.* recognise the impact their high level of emotional need can have on them as people, as well as on their adopted children and potential future children. They also note the impact complex emotional needs can have on the quality of contact with their adopted children, via letterbox, social media or later as young adults. They warn against underestimating the impact their emotional needs can have on future children. Nolte *et al.* argue that understanding and supporting the psychological and emotional needs of birth parents not only helps them and their children, but could also be viewed as a preventative intervention.

The literature review highlights that birth parents are a much marginalised group in society and have often faced many challenges before becoming a parent and prior to any care proceedings. In addition, research indicates that their mental health and wellbeing are further negatively affected by the loss of their children. This is often compounded by many practical problems they also have to face linked to poverty, limited education and employment opportunities. All of this is considerably impacted by the social stigma that birth parents can experience as a result of their child being removed from them and placed for adoption.

The literature notes the many barriers for birth parents to engage in support and the challenges this then places on services to provide support that is accessible to the people who need it.

This chapter then importantly considers the literature regarding what birth parents themselves find useful about support. Independence from statutory services, proactive outreach and accessibility are all noted as factors valued by birth parents. Additionally high on the list is the importance of the therapeutic relationship, one that is nurturing and empathetic, enabling trust to be built.

Exploration of different types of therapeutic support including individual therapy, group support, couples therapy and psychotherapeutic interventions are then also explored.

Chapter 2: 'Like a Light in the Dark': A Hertfordshire University Evaluation of the Adoptionplus Birth Relative Counselling Service

Chapter 2 focuses on Hertfordshire University's independent evaluation of the Adoptionplus Birth Relative Counselling service model. It takes its title 'Like a Light in the Dark' from feedback from a birth mother, involved in the study, describing how she felt about the support she had received. Adoptionplus describe their model as a relationship-based, trauma- and attachment-informed approach to therapeutic support to birth relatives. The model places great emphasis on the provision of a flexible, non-shaming service that encourages and promotes improved reflective functioning and understanding. The Adoptionplus model recognises the value of longer term counselling for some people and a more proactive approach to engagement.

Lizette Nolte, Hannah Wright, Hannah Morgan and Caoimhe Forbes undertook a qualitative and quantitative evaluation of the Adoptionplus model, examining data and interviewing birth parents. When examining those referred to the service they noted the high level of need of this group. Nearly a third were reported to have a learning disability, another third were thought to have a mental health difficulty, whilst 10 per cent were identified as having a personality disorder. Almost half of birth mothers and a quarter of birth fathers were reported to have been abused as children, the most common form of abuse being sexual abuse. In adulthood many birth mothers were additionally also victims of domestic abuse. Nolte *et al.* believe that this high level of trauma was probably under-estimated, with the true prevalence of difficulties likely being much greater.

Nolte *et al.* also noted that engaging with birth relatives offered many challenges, with the stage of adoption process being one factor, as take-up rates were noticeably lower when people were early on in the adoption process. Additionally, the Local Authority contract also seemed to influence take-up, with engagement being much higher where the Local Authority placed no limits on the number of counselling sessions available to each individual. This is understandable when thinking about it from the birth parent's perspective. Why would someone even want to start to open the lid and try and unpick layer upon layer of trauma, if they knew they only had six sessions with a therapist? It makes sense that they would need the reassurance of longer term support if necessary, before they felt safe enough to engage in therapy. The variety of contracts Adoptionplus had with different Local Authorities around England, enabled Nolte *et al.* to identify which approaches were more likely to promote positive engagement, with take-up rates ranging from 29 to 65 per cent. This information could be helpful to commissioning authorities when designing tenders for new services.

Particular attention is then paid to the 'pending service' element of the Adoptionplus model, which offers flexibility to birth relatives regarding when they access the offer of help. The Adoptionplus model doesn't have a 'use it or lose it' approach. Instead it enables people to take their time and consider if and when counselling would be right for them. It also enables people to take a break from counselling and come back to it at a time they felt better able to access the therapeutic support being offered. This approach fits within Beth Neil's research, which identified the fact that individual parents benefited from access to support at different times in their adoption journey, with some people wanting support early on, whilst others did not feel ready until much later.

Nolte *et al*'s evaluation identified five main themes from the birth relative experience of the counselling support:

1. The value they placed on the relationship with their counsellor, often being the first time in their lives that they didn't feel so alone, but instead felt safe, not judged and listened to.

2. The relief of having an opportunity to share thoughts and feelings that they had not been able to express ever before.

3. Counselling helped them to make sense of what had happened to their children and the events that led to their children's removal and placement for adoption.

4. Counselling enabled them to make changes, not just to their lives but to their relationship and importantly to how they felt within themselves.

5. Counselling helped them to put themselves back together again.

One birth mother summed it up:

I used to think I was nothing, but now I think I'm something.

Chapter 3: The Hole That is Left: The Pain of Losing Children to Adoption

In Chapter 3 Carole Green, Adoptionplus counsellor, shares her experience of working with birth parents who have had children removed and adopted. Through case studies Green shares the deep emotional pain and constant void many parents talk about suffering.

This chapter explores the deep sense of shame, that runs alongside the loss that some parents experience: feeling they have failed their children and how this can get in the way of enabling them to grieve for their loss and move forward with their lives. This shame isolates people as they feel unable to talk about their children and are unable to separate the situation that resulted in their children being adopted from who they are as people. Green describes some parents as having an overwhelming feeling of being stuck in this agonisingly painful place and not being able to find a way out.

This chapter explores the complexity of the loss and uses individual stories and case studies to illustrate how it is felt in many ways and on many levels. Green describes the deep emptiness parents feel when explaining this very particular feeling of grief and looks at some of the different ways that birth parents find to start to process it. She describes the experiences of birthdays and Christmases spent without their children and pain of knowing that they are living another life somewhere else, being cared for by other people.

This chapter later explores some of the many ways in which birth parents attempt to manage these feelings of intense loss and emptiness including getting pregnant again.

Chapter 4: Engagement, Flexibility and Pre-counselling

Chapter 4 focuses on the challenge of engaging people in the counselling process who have so many reasons not to want to engage in therapy. Patricia Downing and Joanne Alper share information about the Adoptionplus model and how it is designed to support and enable people to access the services. By sharing case studies they provide an insight into how service design really can make a difference to the accessibility of therapy to this high-need group.

This chapter considers the enormously challenging early lives of many birth parents and the difficulties this leaves them with that can often result in them struggling with a range of significant social and emotional difficulties as adults. These difficulties are often compounded by ongoing trauma in adult life, for example involvement in abusive and domestically violent relationships and problems with drugs and alcohol. Alper and Downing explore the difficulties of trust and relationship building in this context and share the Adoptionplus approach used to address this. They stress the importance of developing a therapeutic service that is flexible in how it engages with people, non-shaming in how it communicates with people and which has the therapeutic relationship at its heart.

This chapter considers the Adoptionplus 'pending' service, which enables flexibility of approach with regard to service engagement and take-up. As opposed to a 'one-time-only', 'use-it-or-lose' it approach, this service is available for people for a number of months should they feel ready to access it. Additionally, a proactive outreach style enables parents whose children have been adopted, to feel 'held in mind' and their welfare thought about, whilst at the same time giving them the opportunity to adjust to the idea of counselling.

This flexibility continues into the counselling provision where Eversol's (1997) description of 'Bending the Frame' is used to highlight the importance of an adaptable and responsive approach to individual therapeutic needs.

This consideration of and sensitivity to the individual is also explored via the thoughtful use of language within their correspondence. Letters and texts are written in a non-shaming and warm manner, even when people are having difficulties attending appointments. These little touches appear to make a positive difference to birth parents.

Chapter 5: Working with Birth Fathers

In Chapter 5 Ian Orr-Campbell, counsellor with the Adoptionplus Counselling Service, provides an insight into his work with birth fathers whose children have been adopted. We have already heard in Chapter 1, that there is a national challenge with engagement of birth fathers in support services. This chapter aims to present information with regard to a therapeutic approach that supports and identifies ways of working with men, which takes into consideration the impact on them of feelings of shame and anger.

In this chapter Orr-Campbell shares case examples to explain his approach to working with birth fathers, who can often present as very angry and hostile. He emphasises the importance of staying connected to the emotion underneath the behaviour and recognising the pain and the shame often hidden by the anger. Orr-Campbell promotes an approach that focuses on attunement to the person and encourages an attitude of curiosity. Additionally he stresses the importance of boundaries in helping to create feelings of safety in the therapeutic relationship, which is essential before any meaningful work can be undertaken. He also emphasises the value of a 'present moment focus' in therapy, to enable the men he works with to shift their perspective and understanding of their feelings and of their situation.

Chapter 6: 'No Quick Fix': The Benefits of Longer Term Counselling for Birth Parents with Complex Histories of Trauma and Abuse: Carrie's Story

In Chapter 6, Dr Kim S. Golding and Jane Gould explore the importance of longer term counselling when working with birth parents with complex histories of trauma and abuse. Gould shares information about Carrie, a birth mother with a significant trauma history, who over a number of years had five children removed and placed for adoption. Gould details Carrie's painful and difficult early childhood and goes on to describe the circumstances that led to the removal of her children.

Golding provides therapeutic commentary of Carrie's experiences and the impact they are likely to have had on her from a Dyadic Developmental Psychotherapy (DDP) perspective. Golding explains how these experiences can impact on Carrie's ability to access and utilise therapy, the impact they have on trust and relationship building, and their links with anger and shame. In essence this chapter explains why short term therapies do not work for people with significant and multiple complex trauma histories and why a longer term approach is more effective.

Chapter 7: 'Contact' from the Birth Parents' Perspective

In Chapter 7 Carole Green, counsellor with the Adoptionplus Counselling Service, provides an insight into the emotions and experience of contact from the birth parents' perspective. Green includes three areas for discussion identified as important by parents themselves during counselling:

- the birth parent's final contact with their child prior to adoption
- meeting their child's future adopters for the first time
- contact via letter exchange once their child has been adopted.

First Green shares the emotional experience of the final meeting with their child prior to adoption. Through Louise, Gary, Jenny, Selina, Gail and Sophie we start to better understand the complex range of emotions and challenges that birth parents face during this monumental moment in their lives and in the lives of their children. How, without support, they are expected to make this overwhelmingly difficult experience as okay as possible for their children, when they don't even know how to make it okay for themselves. To cry or not to cry... Which would be more harmful for their child? To feel overwhelmed by their parent's pain or see them as not caring about saying goodbye... Which is worse? Without support birth parents are left to try and manage this and a multiple number of other emotions and difficulties alone. Green stresses the essential importance of providing support for birth parents before, during and after these very difficult contacts.

The chapter then moves on to share birth parent's experiences of meeting their child's adoptive parents for the first time and again the range of challenging emotions this can evoke. Jasmine's story is especially poignant, where she reaches out and asks her father the day before the meeting to come with her as she is incredibly anxious about doing this on her own. Jasmine tells Green that, although he agreed to support her, he'd been drinking and forgot to come and so she was left to manage alone.

Lastly Green explores contact via letter exchange, often called letterbox contact. For many professionals working in the field of adoption, it may not be something that they often consider from the parent's perspective. However, when you hear Gary's story and the impact that waiting for a letter from his daughter has on him, you can't help but realise the very deep and complex emotions connected to these letters.

Chapter 8: Breaking the Cycle: An Approach to Group Work with Birth Mothers

In Chapter 8 Daljit Gill and Bethany Lambert share information with regards to After Adoption's 'Breaking the Cycle' programme for birth mothers. They start by explaining the benefits of group work programmes and clarify how they have developed their approach, which starts with one-to-one support before moving into group work. They inform us that this model also provides practical support if needed, for example help with travel costs. Gill and Lambert go on to explain that their approach is to provide an empathetic, non-judgemental, trauma-informed and strengths-based service for birth mothers. As with other contributors in this book, they too stress the importance of flexibility within their model and also reference Eversol's 'Bending the Frame' (1997) approach to therapeutic support. This programme includes group discussion, case studies, craft work and multi-sensory activities. Gill and Lambert conclude their chapter with information about Coram's evaluation of this model.

Chapter 9: Taking a Pause: An Innovative Approach to Working with Women Who Have Experienced Multiple Removals of Children

In Chapter 9 Ellen Marks and Sophie Humphreys describe the Pause model and its approach to supporting women who are at risk of repeatedly having children removed. The aim of their model is to support women effectively, so that fewer children come into the care system. Case examples are used, like that of Clara who had nine children removed, to explain how the approach works. Crucial to the Pause approach is the belief in the central importance of the relationship. In fact they describe the relationship as the intervention. The Pause model is about supporting women to build healthy relationships. Marks and Humphreys also believe building safety in the relationship with the Pause practitioner and ensuring that the women feel 'held in mind' are important in the approach they take. As in the previous chapter, Marks and Humphreys also stress the importance of flexibility in their model, stating that they made a deliberate decision when establishing Pause, not to take a manualised approach. Although they describe the Pause approach as therapeutic they are careful to explain that it does not include clinical therapy. They acknowledge that, although many of the women they work with could benefit from longer term specialist clinical treatment, there aren't enough specialist services currently available in the UK that provide the support needed, in the way it is needed.

Conclusion

Finally, Dr Karen Treisman draws together all the key themes and messages in the book, looking at how they link together and are related to the wider social care systems.

Effectively supporting birth parents offers multiple benefits to many. Ruth's open letter at the end of this chapter highlights her own experience as an adoptive mum, of the benefits of therapeutic support to the birth mother of her daughters. Not only did the support really help her, the subsequent relationship they now all have is helping them all.

Final thoughts

This book aims to spotlight the needs of birth parents, who have for decades been much neglected and marginalised. With better understanding of their needs and more effective support, they are more likely to offer a positive contribution to the lives of their adopted children and any future children they may have. A new approach to support for birth parents may challenge policy makers, commissioners and service providers to rethink current practice. Significant change can be challenging, but in these situations I take inspiration from the words of Arthur Ashe, 'Start where you are. Use what you have. Do what you can.'

Why therapeutic adoption support for birth parents matters: An adoptive mum's experience

I'm an adoptive mum with two wonderful daughters. When my girls first came to live with me they really struggled to make sense of their past.

As with many adopted children, my girls, Mia and Alyssia, felt the pain of missing their birth family. They had many worries about their birth family, particularly whether they were okay and if they had forgotten them. Having their birth mum back in their lives has been extremely helpful for them, Mia describes seeing her birth mum as filling a part of her that was missing and Alyssia says she doesn't feel alone anymore. Through contact, their birth mother has been able to answer questions Mia and Alyssia had and helped to build their sense of identity with family information and stories. The girls have been reassured they were and continue to be, loved by their birth family. This has helped secure their place within our adoptive family and helped ease their anxiety of further loss being around the corner.

Their birth mum has been able to be part of our lives, following receiving specialist therapeutic support. Being heard and having her pain acknowledged by caring and passionate workers in a Birth Mums project was a huge part in her starting to heal from everything she'd been through that led to the girls being removed and the unimaginable pain of losing her children. The programme helped her to find strength she didn't know she had and in turn, helped her become part of our family. The therapeutic support she received not only helped her but it has helped our girls too.

Ruth

Part I

Evaluation of Therapeutic Support for Birth Parents (Hertfordshire University)

Chapter 1

How Best to Support Birth Relatives: What the Experts Say

Lizette Nolte, Hannah Morgan and Caoimhe Forbes

I feel like,

I am nothing!

Just a suitcase!

Getting passed on!

Introduction

In the UK, the 2002 Adoption and Children Act increased birth relatives' rights to support services when their children are adopted (Department of Education, 2014). In line with this, the Department of Education (2014), in their document *Adoption: National Minimum Standards*, states that there is a duty to consider the welfare of all parties in the adoption process; that is the child, the adopting family and also the birth relatives. This document goes on to specify that there is a requirement to provide support and counselling for birth parents and other relatives, before, during and after adoption. It is therefore now a legal requirement for Local Authorities to provide independent counselling and support to birth relatives where adoption may be the plan and Local Authorities are inspected on this area of work as part of their Ofsted inspection.

Yet, there is much evidence that these guidelines are not being consistently implemented and birth relatives' needs are not being met (Lindley, Richards & Freeman, 2001; Slettebø, 2013). While there is a powerful and necessary focus on protecting children within the UK child protection system, birth relatives and their wellbeing continue to be neglected. Where there are initiatives to support birth relatives, we know very little about whether these interventions work and whether birth relatives find them helpful. Therefore, there is an urgent need to implement the government's standards for supporting birth relatives more comprehensively and thoughtfully to meet birth relatives' needs (Broadhurst & Mason, 2013). Yet, staff involved in child safeguarding have said that they lack knowledge about the psychological and emotional needs of birth relatives, making it difficult for them to know what support is needed or how best to offer it (Marsh, Browne, Taylor & Davis, 2019).

In this chapter we take a national and international view of what is known about what the psychological and emotional needs of birth relatives are. We then look at what is known about the counselling and support services that currently exist for birth relatives and what we know about whether these services work. Finally, we highlight some important themes to consider when working with birth relatives.

What are the psychological and emotional needs of birth relatives?

It is very important that we understand what the mental health and wellbeing needs of birth parents are. This is not only because of birth parents' own 'deep emotional and practical needs' (Frame, Conley & Berrick, 2006, p.517), it is also because birth relatives often continue to have contact with their children after they have been removed and so can continue to influence the wellbeing of their children (e.g. Battle, Bendit & Gray, 2014; Claridge, 2014; Slettebø, 2013). Also, many birth parents go on to have further children, often getting caught in recurrent care proceedings (Cox *et al.*, 2017) and birth parents continue to have parenting relationships if not with their own children, then with step-children and children in their extended family (Battle *et al.*, 2014; Lewis-Brooke *et al.*, 2017). Therefore, support services for birth relatives can be argued to be a preventative intervention.

A moving early study in the field called *Half a Million Women* by Howe, Sawbridge and Hinings (1992) raised our awareness about birth mothers' painful experiences of broken relationships and loss, urging us to take note of birth relatives' needs. Janette Logan (1996) and Charlton, Crank, Kansara and Oliver (1998) then followed this up to reveal the ongoing pain and deep grief that many birth mothers experience. More recently, researchers and practitioners like Karen Broadhurst and Claire Mason (Broadhurst & Mason, 2013, 2017; Broadhurst *et al.*, 2015), Elsbeth Neil and her colleagues (Neil, 2013; Neil *et al.*, 2010) and others (e.g. Askren & Bloom, 1999; Baum & Burns, 2007; Marsh *et al.*, 2019; Memarnia *et al.*, 2015), as well as charities such as the Family Rights Group (Lindley & Richards, 2002) have helped us understand the emotional, psychological, social and practical needs of birth relatives. Researchers have mostly focused on birth mothers, while birth fathers and the extended birth family have often been neglected. In this section, what we currently know from the literature about the needs of birth relatives will be summarised.

Quality of life, life opportunities and wellbeing

Birth parents often live with numerous day-to-day challenges – they are often living in poverty and have limited education and employment opportunities. They often have intellectual disabilities or are coping with mental health problems or substance misuse difficulties. Very often there is a history of trauma across many generations, including cycles of domestic violence and abuse. These factors can have a powerful impact on birth relatives' quality of live, life opportunities and wellbeing. Things that can potentially protect birth relatives, such as having a good support network from family and the local community, are often missing.

The impact of care proceedings

In addition to these pre-existing challenges, birth relatives are also described as having many emotional and psychological needs due to their experiences of care proceedings and the loss of their children to care or adoption. Birth parents often experience care proceedings as adversarial and traumatic and they describe a lack of compassion and kindness. There is also often a lack of communication and information-sharing. Parents can feel helpless and powerless to influence the situation. These factors can have a negative effect on birth parents' mental health.

A common theme across all the papers reviewed was one of intense loss. Losing a child to adoption is a momentous experience in a birth parent's life. Their sense of loss and grief can be long term and will most likely stay with them for the rest of their lives. Grieving this loss is complicated by the fact that the grief is ambiguous (in that the child is still alive) and also disenfranchised (Doka, 1989) (in that there is a societal belief that birth parents brought the loss on themselves and therefore their grief is not legitimate). This can lead to ongoing, unresolved grief. Many other powerful emotions are common for birth relatives in response to care proceedings. These include feelings of shock, disbelief, anger, guilt, shame, regret and deep emotional pain. These powerful feelings can be difficult to manage and could be expressed in ways that others find challenging. Parents can at times disconnect and separate themselves from such overwhelmingly painful feelings or try to manage their distress through, for example, substance misuse.

Post-removal challenges

Post-removal, birth relatives continue to face many challenges and the literature highlights that these can be lifelong. The ongoing relationship with their children is one such challenge. Many birth parents maintain contact with their children, either through visits or letterbox and this can be particularly painful (while often also rewarding) for parents. Elsbeth Neil and her colleague (Young & Neil, 2004) have highlighted that a number of problems can make contact very challenging for parents, for example they might worry about how contact will affect their child and they might struggle with the restrictions and rules related to contact. Over time it can become harder to feel that they know their child well and therefore finding the right words and topics for conversation can be hard. For parents with a learning disability or low educational attainment, literacy can be an obstacle when having to write a letter.

Post-removal, parents can also face a number of practical problems. Recently Karen Broadhurst and Claire Mason (Broadhurst & Mason, 2017) powerfully highlighted the wider implications of child removal for the lives of parents. Frequently parents whose children are removed from their care are lone parents and dependent on welfare benefits for their income. The loss of welfare benefits and also, if they are dependent on social housing, the loss of housing entitlements, can cause a crisis and increase day-to-day stress. Broadhurst and Mason have referred to this as 'legal stigmatisation' (p.42) and argue that this can reinforce these parents' social marginalisation.

The impact of social stigma is a theme highlighted across all the papers that were reviewed. Stigma can affect every area of a parent's life, from relationships with family, neighbours and friends to meeting of new acquaintances, where especially women will often be asked whether they have children. These parents can be 'categorised as a bad person' (Marsh *et al.*, 2019, pp.e5, e11) by society. Parents can experience intense shame because of this and avoid letting anyone know about the loss of their children in fear of being judged, thereby foregoing potential social support. Also, parents often lose a lot of self-confidence and can see themselves as having what Howe *et al.* (1992) described as a 'spoiled identity'. This can have a wide impact on the lives of birth parents. In particular, mothers can find themselves in repeated cycles of destructive or abusive relationships, succumb to substance abuse or seek solace in a further pregnancy, only to enter an ongoing cycle of subsequent removals.

To summarise, birth relatives can be seen as a 'marginalised and vulnerable group' (Cossar and Neil, 2010) and the removal of their children can have a substantial and multi-layered long-term impact on their quality of life, life choices, mental health and wellbeing.

Are we supporting birth relatives?

Based on what we know about the needs of birth relatives as described above, Karen Broadhurst and Claire Mason (2013) recommend having a clear, proactive protocol for supporting birth relatives. Unfortunately, this remains the exception, rather than the rule (Broadhurst and Mason, 2017; Cossar and Neil, 2010). Elsbeth Neil and her colleagues (Neil *et al.*, 2010) found that only a minority of birth relatives had received specialist mental health services. Neil (2006) also found very few of the birth relatives she interviewed had received any support to deal with the removal of their children. Those who did seek help from mainstream mental health 'talking therapies' reported that adoption issues were not discussed and therefore they had not found the support helpful.

Cossar and Neil (2010) found that, whilst Local Authorities in England and Wales were reasonably good at commissioning and referring to independent support services, they were less successful at monitoring whether the services were managing to engage birth relatives or to monitor the quality of these services. Although interventions have been proposed in the literature, little is known about whether they work. This indicates the urgency of robust evaluations of existing interventions (see Chapter 2 evaluating the Adoptionplus model as an example of this).

What do we know about the support there is for birth relatives?

It is important that we understand what birth relatives value and find useful about support and also what works – here we will discuss what the literature tells us.

Engagement

Before we discuss specific interventions, the matter of engagement will be discussed. This is because the challenge of engaging birth relatives is highlighted as important across the literature we reviewed. There is much discussion of the many barriers to overcome for birth relatives to engage in post-child removal support (e.g. Battle *et al.*, 2014; Cossar and Neil, 2009; Harris, 2005; Hess and Williams, 1982; Jackson, 2000; Koch, 1987; Neil *et al.*, 2010). From the perspective of the service or practitioner, difficulties in engaging birth relatives were at times explained in terms of the birth relatives' 'deficiencies'. Birth relatives were often described as 'hard to reach' or 'difficult to engage'. This leaves the responsibility to engage at the door of birth relatives.

Others, however, have highlighted the many potential barriers faced by birth relatives when seeking support. A number of emotional barriers were emphasised. First, a sense of shame can be an obstacle to seeking help. Birth relatives may have strong feelings of unworthiness and guilt and may fear being judged for failing as a parent (Neil, 2006; Scourfield & Hendry, 1991; Slettebø, 2013). Secrecy can also be an obstacle to engagement, for instance where women avoid support for fear of family members finding out about a historical adoption (Lewis-Brooke *et al.*, 2017).

The relationship with official services or those in authority can also be a barrier and trust can be difficult because birth relatives might feel betrayed or angry, having experienced the removal of their child against their will (Battle *et al.*, 2014; Cox *et al.*, 2017; Deykin, Campbell & Patti, 1984; Harris, 2004, 2005; Higgins *et al.*, 2014; Lewis-Brooke, 2017; Neil, 2006; Sellick, 2007; Smith, 2006). Harris (2005) identified a number of specific barriers to engagement that people of colour might experience, which included a lack of knowledge about what support is available, racist attitudes of staff and the support services themselves being inappropriate for this client group. Despite these barriers to engagement, birth relatives do take up services when the right services are offered by the right agencies at the right time (Lewis-Brooke *et al.*, 2017; Neil, *et al.*, 2010).

Therapeutic relationship

Once birth relatives are engaged with a service, the relationship between birth relatives and practitioners was seen as crucial across all the papers (e.g. Battle *et al.*, 2014; Cox *et al.*, 2017; Harris, 2004; Lewis-Brooke *et al.*, 2017; Slettebø, 2013). All the authors described the same aim – to develop a trusting therapeutic relationship, so that birth relatives can make full use of the service. It is important to create a homely and nurturing therapeutic environment that feels safe to birth relatives and where they feel accepted, cared for and kept in mind. A relationship based on empathy, acceptance, respect, choice and critical friendship is recommended (also see Chapter 2 evaluating the Adoptionplus model for more on this aspect). Harris (2005) warned against creating unrealistic expectations about the service (e.g. that it can help birth parents regain care of their children), as that can break trust.

Interventions

When searching the limited national and international literature describing or evaluating interventions for birth relatives, we found papers describing work carried out in the UK, USA, Australia and Norway. Therapy, counselling or support was offered by practitioners from various fields, including psychologists, social workers, counsellors and psychiatrists, and sometimes birth mothers co-facilitated interventions. The interventions included:

- individual or group support (Cox *et al.*, 2017; Frame *et al.*, 2006; Harris, 2004, 2005; Lewis-Brooke *et al.*, 2017; Robinson, 2002)

- group therapy (e.g. Battle *et al*, 2014; Hess & Williams, 1982; Jackson, 2000; Scourfield & Hendry, 1991; Slettebø, 2013)

- couple therapy (Claridge, 2014)

- psychodynamic therapy (Koch, 1987).

Individual or group support

The intervention most often described in the literature was support services. This covered a wide range of interventions, including direct or telephone counselling (Harris, 2004, 2005); support groups for birth relatives (Harris, 2004, 2005); peer support (Frame *et al.*, 2006) and self-help groups (Robinson, 2002); and, finally, close and intensive partnership working between birth mothers and workers (Cox *et al.*, 2017; Lewis-Brooke *et al.*, 2017).

Authors saw a number of benefits for birth relatives who used support services, including an opportunity to grieve and a sense of relief and freedom that can come with this (Robinson, 2002); developing hope for the future (Lewis-Brooke *et al.*, 2017); social support and friendship (Frame *et al.*, 2006; Lewis-Brooke *et al.*, 2017); and establishing a safe and stable environment for moving on (Frame *et al.*, 2006; Harris, 2004). Authors reported that those who used these support services felt a sense of empowerment, an increase in self-esteem and improvements in parenting skills (Frame *et al.*, 2006). They also said that birth relatives felt they could make more positive decisions in relation to romantic relationships. Some papers reported that more birth parents found work and fewer birth mothers had a further pregnancy (Cox *et al.*, 2017; Lewis-Brooke *et al.*, 2017). However, Frame *et al.* (2006) emphasised that many of their clients also experienced setbacks during their engagement with the service. This possibly points to the importance of longer term interventions for this client group, as well as the possibility for 'top up' sessions following the end of therapy (see Chapter 2 evaluating the Adoptionplus model for more on this). Harris (2004) also noted that these services were mostly focused on birth mothers and that there were no specific support services available for fathers, siblings or extended family members.

It is encouraging that a number of the interventions were developed and/or delivered by or in collaboration with birth relatives or obtained direct feedback from birth relatives of their views of the intervention (Cox *et al.*, 2017; Frame *et al.*, 2006; Harris, 2004, 2005; Lewis-Brooke *et al.*, 2017; Robinson, 2002). However, it is important to note that mostly evaluations were anecdotal and some services were in the early stages of development so more evidence is needed to be sure about the benefits of these interventions.

Group interventions

Group interventions were for birth mothers (Jackson, 2000; Scourfield & Hendry, 1991), birth parents (Battle *et al.*, 2014; Hess & Williams, 1982) or birth parents with social workers and foster parents (Slettebø, 2013). The type of group varied from structured, closed groups to more open-ended, unstructured groups. Battle *et al.* (2014) offered 18 hours of group work over six weeks and addressed issues of shame, isolation, stigma and grief. They also explored parents' values and strengths. Hess and Williams (1982) offered a six-week programme of psycho-education, exploration of emotional responses and support with decision-making. Jackson (2000) and Slettebø (2013) offered open-ended, unstructured groups to facilitate support and reflection.

Overall, all the authors of the papers reported that the group interventions had been helpful. Hess and Williams (1982) reported that relationships between birth parents and case workers improved during the intervention. Slettebø (2013) reported that the group format offered a sense of empowerment; and both Slettebø (2013) and Jackson (2000) highlighted the value of gaining social support and developing friendships. Jackson (2000) also reported that emotions were expressed and thus calmed by the group experience. Battle *et al.*(2014) stated that the group work allowed for grief, shame and stigma to be addressed.

Again, it is encouraging that a number of the group interventions were developed in collaboration with birth relatives or asked for direct feedback from birth relatives (Battle *et al*, 2014; Jackson, 2000; Slettebø, 2013). However, again most of the interventions were in the early stages of development. Also, most were small pilot studies and mostly responses on which the findings were based were anecdotal (Hess & Williams, 1982; Jackson, 2000).

Couples therapy

Claridge (2013) says that adoption causes relationship trauma and therefore suggests that couples therapy is a useful approach. This intervention aims to empower birth parents and create a safe space for processing of the emotional impact of losing a child to adoption or fostering. Small but important benefits were found, suggesting the possible helpfulness of couples counselling. It is important to note that this intervention comes from the USA where voluntary relinquishment is more common. In the UK, couples therapy is not often considered appropriate.

Psychotherapeutic intervention

Koch (1987) describes a re-parenting in the therapeutic relationship with a birth parent in a paper based on a single case study. A psychodynamic model of a parent–child relationship is proposed for therapeutic work with this client group. However, no conclusions can be drawn about the overall usefulness of this intervention.

UK initiatives

In 2012 a small group of practitioners in the UK began to meet to think about the problem of the successive removal of infants in care proceedings and how best to support families for whom this was a reality (Shaw *et al.*, 2014). Since then a number of grassroots initiatives have emerged, for example the 'Pause' project (see Chapter 9); and the Tavistock's Family Drug and Alcohol Court. However, Shaw *et al.* (2014, p.1286) say 'the challenge [is] to move from a proliferation of "grassroots" initiatives to a national strategy and [that] much more research [is] required'.

What should work with birth relatives focus on?

In addition to the types of interventions described above, the literature also highlights some of the specific matters birth relatives might value focusing on in the work with their therapist or counsellor.

Who am I now and how do I go forward?

Many authors (Cox *et al.*, 2017; Harris, 2004, 2005; Hess & Williams, 1982; Jackson, 2000; Lewis-Brooke *et al.*, 2017; Robinson, 2002) highlight the considerable adjustment birth relatives have to make when a child is removed and the uncertainty and confusion they can feel in terms of their relationship with their child and their own identity. Parents' hopes that they might get their children back can often continue and be hard to deal with for birth relatives. Despite children no longer living with parents, parents often very much hold children in mind and worry about them and their wellbeing (e.g. parents worry that children will be given untrue information about them, that their children will forget them, that the child's name might change or that they may not have pride in their cultural background; or worry about how they are influenced e.g. by events on the news). Also, parents can feel uncertain of their role, once their children are removed, with no guidance about how to be a parent without a child, and may need help to adjust to this new role. Birth relatives might need support with managing difficult dates, like birthdays or Christmas. Parents can also need emotional and practical support with establishing and managing contact with their children, as well as with 'coming out' and telling people about their circumstances.

How do I cope with my sense of loss and grief?

Another powerful theme when working with birth relatives found in the literature was loss and bereavement. Grief for birth relatives can often be complex, disenfranchised and not socially validated (Battle *et al.*, 2014; Claridge, 2013; Cox *et al.*, 2017; Frame *et al.*, 2006; Lewis-Brooke *et al.*, 2017; Robinson, 2002). Therefore, there can be some relief for parents when they are encouraged to talk about their loss. Specific interventions, like making life story books, can be helpful to parents in managing their grief.

What do I do when emotions overwhelm me?

In addition to a deep sense of loss, authors also highlight other emotions that might feel quite overwhelming for birth parents. These emotions include anger, bitterness, powerlessness, guilt, regret, shame, uncertainty, emptiness, distress, fearfulness, sadness or relief (Battle *et al.*, 2014; Frame *et al.*, 2006; Harris & Whyte, 1999; Hess & Williams, 1982; Jackson, 2000). When parents feel overwhelmed by such feelings it can not only impact their quality of life, but also their relationships, including their relationship with their child. Respectful witnessing and emotional support to process and make sense of these feelings might be important. Also, working with birth relatives to develop skills and strategies for regulating their emotions might give them more of a sense of control.

How can I feel less alone?

Many birth relatives find themselves socially isolated (Battle *et al.*, 2014; Slettebø, 2013). Helping birth relatives to manage issues of trust can help to overcome such isolation. Also, meeting other women in similar circumstances, where they can discuss their experiences, support one another and make friends can be very useful (Brooke *et al.*, 2017; Claridge; 2013; Frame *et al.*, 2006; Harris, 2004; Harris & Whyte, 1999; Logan, 1996; Neil, 2017; Slettebø, 2013). Offering social activities or hobbies for birth parents can be a practical way to lessen isolation (Neil, 2017).

How do I respond when others blame or judge me?

Birth parents describe experiencing public humiliation and stigma when their children are removed (Higgins *et al.*, 2014; Jackson, 2000; Robinson, 2002; Slettebø, 2013). Therefore, working with birth parents to help them anticipate and deal with the reactions of other people (e.g. rehearsing or role-playing how to respond in social situations) (Neil, 2017) can be very helpful. Some parents may overcome shame by taking part in public activities such as memorials, days of reflection or action, art exhibitions, activism or advocacy for other birth relatives and other ways of raising awareness of the impact of adoption in the broader community (Slettebø, 2013).

How do I cope with the trauma from my past?

Beyond the matters described so far, which relate directly to the removal of their children, the literature also highlights that for many birth relatives, trauma might need to be central in therapy. The adoption itself could be traumatic (Harris & Whyte, 1999; Robinson, 2002), but also many birth relatives have past experiences of abuse or trauma (Claridge, 2013), as has been highlighted. Trauma work can therefore often be an important part of supporting birth relatives.

How can I rebuild my life?

Practical help is often also seen as important in supporting birth relatives. This can include help with, for example, contact with their children, housing, benefits, education or employment (Frame *et al.*, 2006; Neil, 2017). It can be helpful to work with birth parents to help them develop hobbies, interests, employment, educational opportunities or voluntary work. In addition to helping birth relatives be less isolated, as highlighted above, Slettebø (2013) suggests that involving birth relatives in improving services, advocating for birth relatives or engaging in activism to influence change can also provide a way to rebuild their lives, through restoring or building self-confidence or finding purpose. Finally, developing hope for the future and helping birth relatives to reconstruct their lives and move forward is important.

Aspects to focus on when working with birth relatives

– Who am I now and how do I go forward?

- How do I cope with my sense of loss and grief?
- What do I do when emotions overwhelm me?
- How can I feel less alone?
- How do I respond when others blame or judge me?
- How do I cope with the trauma from my past?
- How can I rebuild my life?

Endings

While engagement is highlighted as a very important matter in the literature, it was surprising to note that far less is said about ending work with birth relatives. Where it is mentioned, it is highlighted as a sensitive and important matter which should be managed thoughtfully (Jackson, 2000). This is an area that requires more attention.

Jackson (2000), Harris and Whyte (1999) and others who facilitated group interventions mentioned that group members reported making good friends and staying in touch with other group members after groupwork ended. Many authors reported changes in their clients by the end of the intervention. However, as Broadhurst and Mason (2013) remind us, what we know so far is mostly anecdotal and we do not as yet know what it is that works best for birth relatives.

Conclusion

Summarising the literature has been a challenge. The published papers are all very different and most only describe the interventions they used without really formally evaluating what they did. There is a small amount of encouraging evidence that some of these interventions may be effective and helpful to birth relatives. However, no systematic evaluations have been published and no conclusions about what therapeutic support birth relatives find helpful can be drawn with any certainty. Also, the voices of birth relatives have not been heard enough about what works for them. Therefore, there is an urgent need for further research into best practice for supporting birth relatives. See Chapter 2 evaluating the Adoptionplus model as an example of such an evaluation.

References

Askren, H.A. & Bloom, K.C. (1999) Postadoptive reactions of the relinquishing mother: A review, *Journal of Obstetric Gynecologic and Neonatal Nursing*, 28(4): 395–400.

Battle, C., Bendit, J. & Gray, R. (2014) Groupwork for parents whose children are in care: Challenges and opportunities, *Australian and New Zealand Journal of Family Therapy*, 35(3): 327–340.

Baum, S. & Burns, J. (2007) Mothers with learning disabilities: Experiences and meanings of losing custody of their children, *Tizard Learning Disability Review*, 12(3): 3–14.

Broadhurst, K. & Mason, C. (2013) Maternal outcasts: Raising the profile of women who are vulnerable to successive, compulsory removals of their children – a plea for preventative action, *Journal of Social Welfare and Family Law*, 35(3): 291–304.

Broadhurst, K. & Mason, C. (2017) Birth parents and the collateral consequences of court-ordered child removal: Towards a comprehensive framework, *International Journal of Law, Policy and the Family*, 31: 41–59.

Broadhurst, K., Shaw, M., Kershaw, S., Harwin, J., Alrouh, B., Mason, C. & Pilling, M. (2015) Vulnerable birth mothers and repeat losses of infants to public care: Is targeted reproductive health care ethically defensible?, *Journal of Social Welfare and Family Law*, 37(1): 84–98.

Broadhurst, K. *et al.* (2015) Connecting events in time to identify a hidden population: Birth mothers and their children in recurrent care proceedings in England, *British Journal of Social Work*, 45(8): 2241–2260.

Charlton, L., Crank, M., Kansara, K. & Oliver, C. (1998) *Still Screaming: Birth Parents Compulsorily Separated from Their Children*. Manchester, NH: After Adoption.

Claridge, A.M. (2014) Supporting birth parents in adoption: A couple treatment approach, *Adoption Quarterly*, 17(2), 112–133.

Cossar, J. & Neil, E. (2010) Supporting the birth relatives of adopted children: How accessible are services?, *British Journal of Social Work*, 40(5): 1368–1386.

Cox, P. *et al.* (2017) Reducing recurrent care proceedings: Initial evidence from new interventions. *Journal of Social Welfare and Family Law*, 39(3), 332–349.

Department of Education (2014) *Adoption: National Minimum Standards*. Retrieved from: www.gov.uk/government/publications/adoption-national-minimum-standards

Deykin, E.Y., Campbell, L. & Patti, P. (1984) The post adoption experience of surrendering parents, *American Journal of Orthopsychiatry*, 54: 271–280.

Doka, K. (1989) (Ed.) *Disenfranchised Grief: Recognizing Hidden Sorrow*. Lexington, MA: Lexington Books.

Frame, L., Conley, A. & Berrick, J. D. (2006) 'The real work is what they do together': Peer support and birth parent change, *Families in Society: The Journal of Contemporary Social Services*, 87(4): 509–520.

Harris, F. & Whyte, N. (1999) Support for birth mothers in a group setting, *Adoption and Fostering*, 23(4): 41–48.

Harris, P. (2004) User views and experiences of post-adoption services: A study of a regional post-adoption agency, *Adoption & Fostering*, 28(2), 50–60.

Harris, P. (2005). Family is family…it does affect everybody in the family: Black birth relatives and adoption support, *Adoption and Fostering*, 29(2): 66–74.

Hess, P. & Williams, L.B. (1982) Group orientation for parents of children in foster family care, *Child Welfare*, 61(7): 456–466.

Higgins, D., Kenny, P., Sweid, R. & Ockenden, L. (2014) *Forced Adoption Support Services Scoping Study: Report for the Department of Social Services by the Australian Institute of Family Studies*. Melbourne: Australian Institute of Family Studies.

Howe, D., Sawbridge, P. & Hinings, D. (1992) *Half a Million Women. Mothers Who Lose Their Children by Adoption*. London: Penguin.

Jackson, J. (2000) Developing a post-adoption groupwork service for non-consenting birth mothers, *Adoption and Fostering*, 24(4): 32–39.

Koch, P.M. (1987). Reparenting in the therapeutic relationship with a birth parent: A case, *Child and Adolescent Social Work Journal*, 4(3–4): 89–96.

Lewis-Brooke, S. *et al.* (2017) Mothers apart: An action research project based on partnership between a local authority and a university in London, England, *Revista De Asistentă Socială*, 3: 1–11.

Lindley, B. & Richards, M. (2002) *Protocol on Advice and Advocacy for Parents (Child Protection).* Cambridge: Centre for Family Research, University of Cambridge. Retrieved from www.frg.org.uk/involving-families/parental-advocacy

Lindley, B., Richards, M. & Freeman, P. (2001) Advice and advocacy for parents in child protection cases – what's happening in current practice?, *Child and Family Law Quarterly,* 13(2): 167–195.

Logan, J. (1996) Birth mothers and their mental health: Uncharted territory, *British Journal of Social Work,* 26(5): 609–625.

Marsh, C.A. *et al.* (2019) Making the hidden seen: A narrative analysis of the experiences of Assumption of care at birth, *Women and Birth,* 32(1): e1–e11.

Memarnia, N. *et al.* (2015) 'It felt like it was night all the time': Listening to the experiences of birth mothers whose children have been taken into care or adopted, *Adoption and Fostering,* 39(4): 303–317.

Neil, E. (2006) Coming to terms with the loss of a child: The feelings of birth parents and grandparents about adoption and post-adoption contact. *Adoption* Quarterly, 10(1): 1–23.

Neil, E. (2013) The mental distress of the birth relatives of adopted children: 'Disease' or 'unease'? Findings from a UK study, *Health and Social Care in the Community,* 21(2): 191–199.

Neil, E. (2017) *Helping birth parents in adoption – A literature review of birth parent support services, including supporting post adoption contact. An expertise for the German Research Centre on Adoption (EFZA),* Technical report, retrieved from: https://www.dji.de/fileadmin/user_upload/bibs2017/Neil_Helping_birth_parents_in_adoption.pdf

Neil, E. *et al.* (2010) *Helping Birth Families: Services, Cost and Outcome.* London: BAAF.

Robinson, E. (2002) Post-adoption grief counselling, *Adoption & Fostering,* 26(2): 57–63.

Scourfield, F. & Hendry, A. (1991) Unfinished business – The experience of a birth mothers' group, *Adoption & Fostering,* 15(2): 36–40.

Sellick, C. (2007) An examination of adoption support services for birth relatives and for post-adoption contact in England and Wales. *Adoption & Fostering,* 31(4): 17–26.

Shaw, M. *et al.* (2014). Recurrent care proceedings: Part 1: Progress in research and practice since the family justice council 6th annual debate. *Family Law,* 44(9), 1284–1287.

Slettebø, T. (2013) Partnership with parents of children in care: A study of collective user participation in child protection services. *British Journal of Social Work,* 43(3): 579–595.

Smith, S.L. (2006) *Safeguarding the Rights and Well-being of Birthparents in the Adoption Process.* New York: Evan B. Donaldson Adoption Institute.

Young, J. & Neil, E. (2004) The 'Contact after Adoption' study: The perspective of birth relatives after non-voluntary adoption. In E. Neil and D. Howe (Eds), *Contact in Adoption and Permanent Foster Care: Research, Theory and Practice* (pp.85–104). London: British Association for Adoption and Fostering.

Chapter 2

'Like a Light in the Dark': A Hertfordshire University Evaluation of the Adoptionplus Birth Relative Counselling Service

Lizette Nolte, Hannah Wright, Hannah Morgan and Caoimhe Forbes

I used to think I was nothing

but now I think I am something

Introduction

As described in Chapter 1, it is essential that there is good research to find out what helps birth relatives, how best we can support them and how birth relatives experience services. This chapter will offer an evaluation of the Adoptionplus Birth Relative Counselling Service.

Adoptionplus has been providing a birth relative counselling service since 2004, using a uniquely developed service structure and approach. Since that time they have worked with nearly 1000 birth relatives with referrals to the service coming from a number of Local Authorities around the UK. Although Adoptionplus received feedback from birth relatives reporting positive changes to their lives as a result of the counselling, the agency wanted a more in-depth understanding of its provision. They approached Hertfordshire University as they wanted to better understand what aspects of their service were effective, why it was effective and how it could be improved.

Adoptionplus service ethos

Adoptionplus take a relationship-based trauma-informed approach to service provision. Flexibility and compassion are central components. They focus on providing a non-shaming, non-judgemental service that encourages people to better understand their past and current situation and make links to the removal of their children. The intention of the service is to provide birth relatives and any future children they may have, the chance of a more positive future. The service often provides one of very few and for some the first ever, experiences of a non-abusive and nurturing relationship. The Adoptionplus qualified and accredited counsellors take an integrative, but largely person centred approach to therapy. In addition, two counsellors are also qualified mindfulness teachers, one counsellor is trained in Eye Movement Desensitisation and Reprocessing (EMDR) and another counsellor is also trained in Sensorimotor Psychotherapy. Counsellors have additionally received training in Dyadic Developmental Psychotherapy.

Adoptionplus service model

The Adoptionplus Birth Relative Counselling Service offers:

- access to longer term counselling if needed, with the recognition that some people will need to 'dip in and out' of counselling at different points during their lives

- pending service to encourage take-up

- flexibility with regards to attending appointments, working with the person's circumstances and 'readiness'

- proactive support with regard to attendance (e.g. through reminder texts or telephone calls)

- availability of phone counselling and face-to-face counselling, depending on what birth parents need and prefer (sometimes both options offered during the course of the therapy)

- supportive organisational culture that promotes the emotional health of its counsellors.

Aims of the evaluation

The aims of the evaluation were to:

- identify who is being referred to the service and how and when they are referred

- see what, if any, differences there are between the birth relatives who take up the service and those who do not

- see how birth relatives move through the service from when they are referred until they end their contact with the service

- explore service users' views of the service and whether and how counselling has been useful to them

- explore referrer views of the service

- explore counsellor views about what matters when working with birth relatives.

What we did

We analysed existing records held by the service, including referral forms, quarterly reports for commissioners and therapists' closing summaries. We also analysed feedback questionnaires completed by birth relatives who used the service and by referrers. Also, we interviewed five birth mothers who received long-term counselling from the service and benefitted from it. Finally, we interviewed four counsellors and a first-contact staff member about their experiences of offering counselling and support to birth relatives.

Who was included

Existing records and questionnaires were for all birth relatives referred to the service over a two-year period, from 1 April 2012 to 31 March 2014. There were 304 eligible referrals during this time, namely 209 mothers, 70 fathers, 22 grandparents, 2 aunts and 1 uncle. Counsellors and first-contact staff were the current staff of the service. The birth mothers who we interviewed were current or recent users of the service. All records were anonymised by Adoptionplus and all information was treated confidentially and will be anonymised here.

What we found

Where did referrals come from?

Referrals came via five different contracts with Local Authorities around England, one of which was a consortium of London Boroughs. The vast majority (over 80%) of referrals came from Local Authority social workers, while the rest were almost all self-referrals. Referrals were made at different stages throughout the adoption process, from early stages to completion and beyond. About a third of referrals were made once placement and/or care orders had been made, which was the most common time to refer, while a quarter of referrals were made during care proceedings. Each Local Authority contract placed different requirements on Adoptionplus service provision. Some contracts placed no restriction on how many therapy sessions could be provided, or stage in the adoption process, although others placed significant restrictions on these areas.

Who was referred to the service?

Birth relatives were most commonly referred individually (about two thirds of referrals). However, some were also referred with their partners or with another family member.

According to referral information, over three quarters of birth relatives referred to the service were white British. Others were described as mixed heritage, white other, black African, black Caribbean, Asian, black British, white Irish or other. Nearly a third of referred birth relatives had or were thought to have a disability. The most common disability was learning disability, with a quarter of all referrals having or suspected of having a learning disability.

Over a third of birth relatives were thought (by the person who referred them) to have mental health difficulties. The most common mental health difficulty was depression, which was reported for one in five birth relatives. Almost one in 10 birth relatives were reported to have a diagnosis, or traits of, a personality disorder. Substance misuse was mentioned in 15 per cent of referrals.

Overall, two in every five birth relatives – including almost half of birth mothers and a quarter of birth fathers – were reported to have been abused as children. The most common form of abuse was sexual abuse. Over a quarter of all birth relatives were reported to have been sexually abused as children; this included more than a third of birth mothers and more than of birth fathers. In adulthood, more than a quarter of birth relatives were reported to have been the victims of domestic abuse; again, mothers were most commonly affected. In total, almost three in five birth relatives were reported to have suffered some form of abuse over the course of their lives, including almost three quarters of birth mothers and nearly a third of birth fathers.

Because the information came from referral forms, most of which were completed by social workers, the mental health difficulties and experiences of abuse reported here are likely to under-estimate the true prevalence of difficulties. Nevertheless, these results demonstrate that birth relatives are a highly vulnerable group, with complex difficulties that are likely to make the experience of losing a child to adoption even harder to bear.

What the birth mothers said

- Rebecca: I was abused as a kid...okay, fair enough, it might affect a little bit about me raising my kids, but obviously I didn't see...

- Elisabeth: It's about all my violent relationships. I felt like I was controlled, that's what she[1] (counsellor) said, I was controlled. She said I was...having bad memories,...about the violence,...and then she turned round and said: he can't hurt you anymore. You know what I mean? I felt really...petrified. But now if I see him, I'm not bothered, you know?

What the counsellors said[2]

- I am working with a client now...and she was abused by her father and then by her maternal uncle as a child. And she said 'no', (but) it wasn't heard. And so there's often those experiences of saying 'no', but either that they are not heard or there being negative consequences for saying no. I just think people feel very frightened. People that have survived childhood by being compliant - because that's the way that they manage to get (their) needs met or manage to not be abused - become very compliant adults.

- When you're thinking about the work, the ability to take responsibility, to... stand back and think 'yeah, these are the bits that went wrong and these are the reasons they went wrong' and understanding (one's) childhood, (one's) ability and...capacity to be a parent, dealing with trauma, I think that takes longer.

---

1   Counsellors will be referred to as 'she' and 'her' throughout for ease of reading and to protect anonymity. Direct quotes have been edited slightly to improve readability, while preserving meaning.

2   Counsellor quotes are unattributed to further protect anonymity.

A range of reasons were stated for the removal of the children. Almost half of referrals stated an inability or lack of capacity to meet the needs of the children. Almost a third stated that the children were neglected and almost a third again stated that there was domestic violence. Around a fifth of referrals stated substance misuse problems. Other reasons given for removal of children included: physical abuse or unexpected injuries, homelessness or insecure housing, prison sentences or involvement in serious crime, emotional abuse, sexual abuse, contact with risky individuals, historic concerns about parenting and voluntary relinquishing.

The number of related children who had been or were being adopted ranged from one to seven. Over a quarter of birth relatives had also lost other children to other forms of alternative care, such as long-term foster care or special guardianship orders. Most birth relatives did not have children living at home; however, a small number did have a child or children living in their home and a further few were expecting a baby.

The take-up of services

The task of winning the trust of birth relatives, who are negotiating an adversarial adoption system and helping them access support, creates many challenges for services. Engaging birth relatives offer many challenges. Previous research (Neil, Cossar, Lorgelly & Young, 2010) has found a low take-up of adoption support services for birth relatives. Cossar & Neil (2009), who surveyed Local Authorities, voluntary adoption agencies and adoption support agencies in England and Wales, identified that low take-up of services was an issue for 90 per cent of respondents. In our research we found that there was a considerable variation in take-up across the five different Local Authority contracts, ranging from 29 to 65 per cent. Take-up was lower in areas where there was a six-session limit on the number of sessions available. It does seem that that birth relatives' awareness of the short-term nature of the counselling impacted on whether they took up the service in the first place. Also take-up was much better where there was no limit and where the counselling location was arranged close to the birth relative's home.

The stage of the adoption process at the time of the referral and how the referral is made seem to be important for whether birth relatives will engage with the service. It has been found in other research that birth relatives who referred themselves to services were more likely to attend and we found the same here. Birth relatives who found themselves later in the adoption process, that is where their children had already been placed with prospective adoptive parents, were more than three times more likely to take up services. Where adoptions had been finalised, birth relatives were 12 times more likely to attend than birth relatives still in the early stages of the process. In areas with the lowest take-up of counselling, the contract required that all referrals could only be made, very early on, prior to the adoption order.

Usually birth fathers have been found to be less likely to take up services and our evaluation showed the same for the Adoptionplus service. Birth relatives who struggled with substance misuse problems were particularly unlikely to engage with services. White British birth relatives were more likely to attend and other researchers have shown that there are specific challenges to engaging with services for birth relatives of colour (Harris, 2005).

Key messages to improve take-up of services

- Do not restrict referrals for counselling support to early on in the adoption process: the right time for counselling for some people might not be until much later.
- Offering longer term counselling will improve engagement - limiting sessions from the start might discourage birth relatives from engaging.
- Offering flexibility in where the counselling takes place and offering counselling in a convenient location close to home will improve engagement.
- Make sure that services are suitable and welcoming for birth relatives of colour.
- Birth fathers and extended family (e.g. birth grandparents) may need a more pro-active approach to encourage them to engage.
- It might be necessary to support birth relatives to address personal difficulties with substance misuse.

Journey through the service
Ways of using the service

Of the birth relatives referred who never attended for counselling (almost 60%), nearly a quarter (24.2%) were never successfully contacted by the service, despite numerous attempts. A third of those referred declined services, while a further third accepted the offer of services, but dropped out before attending a first appointment.

For those who did attend, Neil *et al.* (2010) described different ways in which birth relatives used services – they divided people into either brief service users, who attended one to four appointments, or regular service users, who attended five or more appointments. Table 2.1 shows that more birth relatives were brief service users than were regular service users. The number of appointments attended ranged from 1 to 77 appointments, with the average number of appointments being just under 10 and the most common number of appointments attended being 4.

Table 2.1: Brief and regular service use

Category of service use	%
Brief service user – attended one to four sessions	56
Regular service user – attended five or more sessions	44
Total	100

The 'pending' service

Once referrals have been received, the service offers flexibility in when birth relatives must take up the offer of help. Service users can be held on a 'pending' list at any stage of service use. Overall, the pending system was used for almost three quarters of all referrals. Over half of birth relatives who attended counselling had made use of the pending system at some stage.

There are three categories of pending:

Pending first contact

Simply establishing contact with birth relatives referred to the service is no easy task. When initial attempts to contact are unsuccessful, referrals are not closed. Instead, contact attempts will resume after a set period of time, typically three months and this process can be repeated up to three times. In total, 38 per cent of all birth relatives went through this system.

Pending first appointment

If birth relatives do not wish to engage with counselling at the time they are contacted by the service, they are offered a call-back, typically three months later, so that they will have another opportunity to take up the service at a later time. This process can be repeated several times.

In total, almost a third requested a call-back. Using this system meant that many of birth relatives who did not attend counselling received multiple contacts from the service.

Pending between appointments

If a birth relative requests a break from counselling, or if their attendance becomes irregular, they may be placed on the pending list with a view to resuming counselling at a more suitable time. This is also used when birth relatives have reached the maximum number of sessions offered but would like further counselling if space becomes available; 18 per cent of birth relatives who attended counselling used this service.

What the birth mothers said

- Rebecca: I didn't want to talk to nobody, I didn't want to do anything and (my) social worker said 'you have counselling', it's just like 'no!'...and I was just like 'I've just lost everything! You're asking me to go talk to another complete stranger!' and...I'm just like 'I'm not gonna speak to a complete stranger' and my mum (said) 'just try it, it might work' and I'm like 'how is it going to work?'... It's not gonna get me kids back.' My mum said, 'no, but it's gonna help you understand, get you to a point where it's gonna get you to, hopefully do more than what you're doing'. And obviously the social worker says 'yeah', you know and obviously they put my name down.

- Lara: 'Cos before I'd had people that told me, 'oh I'm working with you' when they weren't... I felt like they were working against me to get evidence to take me kids. So, there's that issue to it as well, so like, (it took me) the first five or six appointments to get to know her (counsellor).

What the counsellors said

- Before we meet this person we have to connect with them in one way or another. Also, I'm quite flexible the way I do that, I'd rather talk to someone straight away, but some people don't want to talk to you, they want to text you and then they want to come and see you.

- It would be [challenging] for people maybe, to trust, to build the relationship, to just organise themselves in the midst of what is going on. Sometimes you get, 'I didn't have the money to get the bus' or...'I had to go to this other appointment at the last minute', or 'I just forgot'. Sometimes I think...it would be a bit punitive, to be honest, to apply some of the kind of boundaries, if you like, that you might normally apply, which could be helpful in other settings... I am not sure that they would be helpful - I think they would be a bit more punitive potentially. They are needing that flexibility, really.

- At times it's like fishing. It's like 'how are you doing? Do you think that you could make it in today? Do you want to make it in? Do you want to talk to somebody?' on the telephone and I have done this before with the aim that eventually you'll bring that person in.

Feedback from birth relatives

Birth relatives completed feedback questionnaires after six sessions of counselling and at similar intervals after that (in total, 118 feedback questionnaires, completed by 46 birth relatives were analysed). Five birth mothers who had used the counselling service and benefitted from it also took part in interviews about the service. In the questionnaires all the participants said that the service was either very helpful or quite helpful. No one who completed the questionnaire said that the service was unhelpful.

All the comments in the questionnaires were analysed for themes. All the interviews were transcribed and also analysed for themes. Across the questionnaires and interviews there were five main themes about what made counselling helpful for the birth relatives.

These were:

- having someone in my corner – building a special relationship

- experiencing a 'release'

- making sense of what happened to my children

- being able to make changes

- putting myself back together.

1. Having someone in my corner-building a special relationship

There was a sense that many birth relatives had felt alone, vulnerable and judged during the removal and adoption of their child, and that the support they received from the counselling service made them feel that there was someone on their side. They felt safe with their counsellor and felt listened to. They felt that their counsellors did not judge them. For many of them, this was in contrast to other relationships, both in their personal lives and with professionals.

What the birth mothers said

Questionnaires

- The only support network I have had, like the 'light in the dark'.
- I feel like I am not judged for my problem.

Interviews

- Isobel: I thought she's [counsellor] lovely, you know, 'cos, when I talk to her she understands and listens. And she was a nice person you see and I like her.
- Rebecca: Knowing that there's someone who's there for you, even when you're in...your darkest days, you've got someone there that's actually willing to talk to you, so yeah, that helps.
- Elisabeth: They make you feel...you're not on your own (pause), they make you feel like, you know, you're the family, you're not, you're not just, like, 'oh, it's you, ok go on that side' they don't make you feel like that. 'Oh yeah, come in! Would you like a cup of tea?' you know they make you feel welcome.

---

2. Experiencing a 'release'

Birth relatives found it helpful to have somewhere to vent and unload. There was a sense that birth relatives valued the opportunity to share thoughts and feelings that they had not been able to express elsewhere and that they felt a sense of relief in opening up. They said they found it helpful to talk and be heard and to be able to express their feelings. For many of the mothers who were interviewed, counselling provided the first opportunity for some feelings to be validated and expressed.

What the birth mothers said

Questionnaires

- [It] helped me to be able to open up, cry, get angry.
- I have been able to talk about the most awful and vulnerable things and [my counsellor] has stayed strong for me which has allowed me to be open about my thoughts.

Interviews

- Rebecca: I found a lot of pressure come off me when I was talking to her [counsellor]. A lot of the pressure I was feeling when I lost the kids, when

I was speaking to her, it felt like a weight was coming off...and all the problems and everything I was going through and the hurt and everything... just speaking (to) her just felt like, well, the weight started coming off my shoulders.

- Isobel: 'Cos it helps me a real big time, a lot, counselling... (I) talk about lots of things, cos it's in my brain you see, I think about everything and then it builds up, builds up and then I've got to let it out.

- Lara: ...it were like a release, so like all that pain and stuff that I'd been through for that 11 years, just wanted to burst, but then I started just coming to see [my counsellor] just for an hour every week...

3. Making sense of what happened to my children

Some birth relatives said that they had used counselling to develop insight into the events that had led to their child's removal and placement for adoption and the situation that they now found themselves in. Counselling was described as a space where intense emotional experiences could be shared and acknowledged.

What the birth mothers said

Questionnaires

- I am more able to make connections between why I feel something - connecting it to particular life events that have happened in my life.
- I am able to talk about my girls without being distressed, enjoy the memories I have with them. I am not afraid to feel whatever emotion comes or fear that it will overwhelm me.

Interviews

- Lara: 'Cos I suppose when you have your baby took off you, you feel like it's you, yeah? But it's not all you. And it's like, I don't know, they help you see that it's not all you.
- Rebecca: ...where it hurts the most you get upset and it really hurts and obviously you tell the counsellor how much it hurts and (about) the pain and everything and the emotional pain and stuff. She can help you heal that by talking to you...she puts it in a way where it doesn't hurt so much. It's coming to more of an understanding and she helps you through that emotional pain.

4. Being able to make changes

Some relatives said that counselling had helped them to develop coping skills that helped them to tolerate the distress and anger they felt and to get on with daily life. Some relatives described making practical changes in their lives, like going out more or getting a job. For others they made changes in their relationships or how they felt within themselves.

What the birth mothers said

Questionnaires

- Helping me keep my anger under control more better. And I feel in my home life it is working and I seem to control it better than before within the last couple of years.

- Helped me to mature, to be able to get on with day to day life, despite everything that is going on.

Interviews

- Elisabeth: They've really helped me with a lot of things, you know, my past, the violence, having my kids taken away from me, you know and now I've got myself a job and I've got myself a new partner - we've been together six years and I'm happy.

- Saffron: It gave me a lot of perspective to sort of stand back and think 'okay, maybe I'm not...as bad, maybe there is a little bit more hope than I thought'.

---

5. Putting myself back together

Some relatives said that they had used counselling to help them to pick up the pieces of their lives and work towards a different future to the one that they had imagined. There was a sense that their old identities had been 'spoilt' or taken away during the removal of their child and placement for adoption and that they now needed to work out who they were, after all that had happened. Particularly, they felt that counselling helped them to feel connected to their absent children and work out how to still be a parent while not having their children with them. For some birth relatives they felt that they were developing confidence and self-worth, finding themselves and their voice and moving forward.

What the birth mothers said

Questionnaires

- You have listened to me, made me feel worth something, improved my self-value.
- I used to think I was nothing, but now I think I am something :-)
- I finally feel I have a right to exist and I've not had that feeling ever before.

Interviews

- Saffron: It's hard to feel loved by your kids sometimes, like if you know you've not got 'em... [becomes tearful] and it's just sort of, you know, picking out bits...so I knew that they cared.
- Rebecca: I still think about you know...what I'd be doing if the kids were there and...you know, about school and I still do think about that... everything's different, cos you're not up early in the morning taking the kids to school, getting them ready, you know, you're not doing meals, you're not...everything's different because...I don't have to do that anymore.
- Lara: ...when I come out from thingy [counselling] I'm like, 'right then, I'm a good person and I'm gonna do this!' [laughs]

Feedback from referring Local Authority social workers

Questionnaires are sent out to referring social workers via Survey Monkey to gain feedback about the referral process and about the value of the service for birth relatives. While return rates of these are too low to make generalisations, the feedback is still valuable.

Overall, referrers resoundingly felt that the referral process was clear and straightforward and that they were very satisfied with the service. For example, referrers appreciated being able to make a telephone referral and liked getting useful information and regular updates from the service.

What the referrers said (questionnaires)

- It's so refreshing that we can make a referral via the telephone. It saves so much time.
- Very happy with the staff, always useful information given and regularly updated.
- Always polite and helpful and flexible to accommodate birth parents' commitments.

However, the questionnaires also showed that often referrers did not know whether the referred birth relative had taken up the service, whether they found it helpful or whether the birth relatives had made any changes in their lives because of the counselling. This was mostly because either they did not have any further contact with the birth relatives after they referred them, or another worker had taken over the work with the family. This fits with what the *Helping Birth Families* research (Neil *et al.*, 2010) found, namely that agencies are often reasonably good at commissioning and referring to birth relative support services, but that they do not check whether birth relatives engage with the services or whether the services are helpful.

For about a third of referrers who did stay in touch with the birth relatives they referred, they overall reported that the service has been very useful, noting particular changes that the birth relatives had made. For example, they felt that birth relatives were accepting their circumstances more, could manage their emotions better or had made some positive changes in their lives. A very small minority said that the birth relatives had not found the counselling useful.

What the referrers said (questionnaires)

Many referrers clearly found that the service benefitted birth relatives, saying e.g.:

– There has been a vast improvement in how some of our birth parents regain control of their lives since attending the counselling sessions. Our families appear less anxious or upset and seem to be able to cope better in their daily routines and lives.

– The service user has been able to come to terms with the adoption of her children and has been able to come to terms with the loss and grief and is able to prioritise the other children's needs that remain in her care. Her sense of guilt and loss is managed more productively.

Feedback from counsellors

Four counsellors and one first-contact staff member were interviewed. The interviews were transcribed and analysed. The following themes were identified:

- building relational trust and hope
- meeting clients where they are

- witnessing changes
- valuing supervision and support
- looking after oneself.

Building relational trust and hope

Counsellors were aware that birth relatives often come from traumatic backgrounds and might not be familiar with more kind and nurturing relationships. They also might have lost trust in those in authority. Therefore, they noticed that they had to go the extra mile to establish connection and that they often held responsibility for maintaining that connection.

What the counsellors said

- ...the service is about bringing the parents on board in a very non-threatening and non-judgemental way and in a way that aims to understand their story and their experience from their perspective. So, rather than us coming from a judgemental 'oh your children have been removed, you've done something really wrong', it's much more about a general enquiry into 'What's happened? What's led you to this point?'
- I think it takes real time to build trust in somebody and really feel that 'yeah, this person doesn't judge me and actually do care about me and (is) not making assumptions about who I am as a person or judging me for the things I might have done wrong'.
- I think they're coming into that service with a distinct lack of trust, I think, around people they've perceived to be in authority.

Meeting clients where they are

Counsellors held an awareness of the often complex and challenging lives birth relatives lived. They therefore felt it was important to follow the client's lead and offer a very flexible service.

What the counsellors said

- I think it is even more of a challenge in this situation, because of people feeling disempowered and I feel aware of that and it's being more flexible (and) following their lead.

> – With this particular type of client, there has to be a flexible approach, because they don't know the rules. They won't sit down and go 'so, here's my problem'. And why should they know the rules? There's so much that's going on in their lives that are chaos and crisis.

Witnessing changes

Counsellors felt privileged to witness many changes that birth relatives made through the process of counselling and these changes felt significant to them, even when small. Counselling was a place where parents could express their challenging feelings, including parenting feelings and where they could make sense of what had happened to them, as well as find a way to move forward.

> **What the counsellors said**
> – How much she changed in terms of how to take responsibility and understand what had gone wrong and why and what she needed to do to be different as a parent this time around.
> – When a client isn't ready for psychological contact, which many of these aren't,…the work then is about helping them have a relationship with you.

Valuing supervision and support

Counsellors described the many challenges of working with birth relatives. The work presented ethical challenges, required a proactive approach that could be demanding and often required thoughtfulness and creativity. Therefore, they particularly valued working for an organisation that understood these challenges. They appreciated a supportive and nurturing working environment, regular supervision, ongoing professional development and training, and caring peer support. Therefore, there was a sense that a trauma-informed, flexible and non-judgemental therapeutic approach need to be mirrored by a similarly informed organisational structure in this line of work. The small ways in which the organisation showed care and held them in mind seemed to be particularly meaningful.

> **What the counsellors said**
> – That's the first thing, knowledge about vicarious traumatisation, the use of supervision and peer group supervision…

- As well as supervision, you've got the team meetings, so you may want to ask people, this is what's happening, what do you guys think, this is what I am thinking, because it's quite complex issues...
- The fact that we meet monthly is really important, really important to me because it means I am part of a team.
- I think they care for their practitioners as much as the practitioners care for their clients.
- They have always had this thing, 'oh let's take care of you guys', so we always get scones at our meetings, that's nice, it's those little touches...it's nice you get a bit of nurture too.

Looking after oneself

Counsellors reported that work with birth relatives could potentially also take a toll on their own wellbeing. Therefore, they emphasised the importance of good self-care, including keeping clear boundaries from between life and work, taking regular time out from work (e.g. holidays), using stress-management strategies (e.g. regular exercise, mindfulness practices, yoga, etc.) and maintaining a good work-life balance (e.g. through time with family and friends, engaging in hobbies, etc.).

What the counsellors said

- You've got a way of kind of taking care of yourself; you've got a way of coming back to the present moment; you've got a way of perhaps connecting with a bit more of an open spacious view of things...which I think is helpful with this work - to see the bigger picture a bit...
- ...(remembering the importance of) being honest with yourself, taking regular holidays and also developing a philosophy of shaking it off, 'okay that's not my stuff, that's your stuff'.
- I do yoga at a yoga class every week...and practising mindfulness a little bit...
- ...and the fact that I have a day off a week and I will never book clients in that space.

Discussion

We have described an evaluation of the Adoptionplus person centred, relationship-based and trauma-informed service for birth relatives. A few areas will now be considered further.

A vulnerable and traumatised client group

In line with previous research (e.g. Neil *et al.*, 2010), this study found that birth relatives are a vulnerable and traumatised group that face many challenges when trying to deal with the grief, loss and anger of losing a child to adoption. The descriptions here do not adequately convey the harrowing life stories the birth relatives reported. The challenge of winning their trust, when services have failed to protect them before, during and after the adversarial care proceedings, is clearly a formidable task. It is possible that earlier intervention may have helped to prevent some of the adoptions in this study.

The right time for counselling

This study found that birth relatives were more likely to engage with counselling towards the end of the adoption process, or after adoptions had been finalised. Neil *et al.* (2010) previously stated that people are able to access counselling at different times. They recommended that adoption panels should routinely ask whether birth relatives have been referred for support. These panels, as well as statutory reviews, may also be an opportunity to provide birth relatives with information about local services at a time when they may be more likely to make use of them. This does not mean that referrals earlier in the process should be deterred. Rather, this highlights the importance of support not offered as a one-off, but rather offered at different stages from the beginning, throughout and after the adoption process. Birth relatives have the right to independent support and the independence of the support offered should be made clear in how the support is introduced to birth relatives.

The value of a flexible service

Where birth relatives are willing to take the risk of engaging with a service, they still face many logistical challenges of getting to counselling. Flexibility in when and how service users access the service is a distinctive feature of this service model. Birth relatives interviewed by Neil *et al.* (2010) welcomed active attempts to convince them to use the service, interpreting it as a sign of care and concern. Such efforts may help to set up the sense of 'having someone in my corner', which was identified as a benefit by service users in this study. Many birth relatives who do not go on to access counselling opt in to the call-back service; for some of them, being kept in mind and reached out to by the service at a time of crisis may in itself be helpful.

Bending the frame

As well as flexibility, birth relatives valued the warm welcome they received, which included for some a 'cup of tea'. Bending the frame (Eversole, 1997) describes a flexible approach to the therapeutic frame which addresses the complex and ever-changing circumstances of the client. In line with the Adoptionplus relationship-focused approach, this might involve, making home visits, providing telephone counselling sessions, becoming an advocate, or for example, helping a relative write a letter to their adopted child. This also involves a 'way of being', with an informal stance that prioritises human connection and unconditional positive regard. For many of the birth relatives in this study, this was a rare and powerful experience.

Recommendations

This evaluation shows that, where birth relatives can be engaged with counselling support services, such services can be helpful to them and allow them to make meaningful changes in their lives. However, some conventions of counselling might have to be left behind, for example by taking responsibility for connection and allowing flexibility around attendance.

Recommendations for commissioners and service developers

- Commissioners should consistently assure that support services are available for birth relatives during and after care proceedings, as well as after an adoption order.
- Adoption panels should routinely enquire whether birth relatives have been referred for independent support and should have information about local services available at meetings.
- Local Authorities should monitor whether services manage to engage the birth relatives they refer and whether the services are helpful to birth relatives.
- Where possible, strict limits on the number of sessions available should be avoided for this client group.

Recommendations for services offering support to birth relatives

– Easy referral pathways (e.g. accepting telephone referrals) is valuable to referrers and could increase referral rates.

– Consider implementing a 'pending' system to provide potential service users with flexibility about when to access help.

– Fathers and birth relatives from ethnic minority backgrounds should be consulted and/or invited to co-produce marketing materials and outreach strategies to encourage self-referrals from these groups.

– Offering to meet with birth relatives near their home should be offered where possible.

– Rather than strictly adhering to traditional counselling boundaries, a warm welcome and a flexible and nurturing approach is likely to promote engagement.

– Regular supervision and continued professional development for counsellors working with birth relatives are important.

– An organisational culture that promotes relationship-based, flexible, non-shaming and compassionate approaches to service provision is sustaining of staff.

Recommendations for further research

– Learning more about what works for this birth relatives is important.

– Further research should be carried out to understand the experiences of birth relatives who do not take up services, who consider counselling, but do not engage, or who start counselling, but drop out early on.

– More research should be carried out to evaluate different forms of support.

Strengths and limitations of the research

Information was collected from five different areas of England over a two-year period and birth relatives' service involvement was followed for a further two-year period. Multiple data sources were used, both quantitative and qualitative (questionnaires and in-depth interviews). Views were included from birth relatives, staff and referrers. No standardised measures were used to collect information on birth relatives' mental health and trauma experiences and birth relatives were not asked directly about these. Information provided by referrers is likely to underestimate the true prevalence of these difficulties. Some voices and views are missing from this research, particularly birth relatives who did not attend counselling, or who dropped out early and those who did not find counselling helpful.

Conclusion

This evaluation has shown that birth relatives can benefit significantly from this particular model of independent person centred counselling. The importance of engagement, flexibility and a safe, consistent and non-judgemental atmosphere was highlighted.

References

Cossar, J. & Neil, E. (2009) Supporting the birth relatives of adopted children; how accessible are services? *British Journal of Social Work*, 40: 1368–1386.

Eversole, T. (1997) Psychotherapy and counselling: Bending the frame. In M. G. Winiarski (Ed.), *HIV Mental Health for the 21st Century* (pp.23–38). New York: New York University Press.

Harris, P. (2005) Family is family…it does affect everybody in the family: Black birth relatives and adoption support, *Adoption and Fostering*, 29(2): 66–74.

Neil, E., Cossar, J., Lorgelly, P.,& Young, J. (2010) *Helping Birth Families: Services, Costs and Outcomes*. London: British Association for Adoption & Fostering.

Part II

A Trauma-Informed and Relationship-Based Approach to Therapeutic Support for Birth Parents (Adoptionplus)

Chapter 3

The Hole That is Left: The Pain of Losing Children to Adoption

Carole Green

It's Christmas time

My beautiful girls

I will miss you so much.

Today my heart ached

with a physical pain

After a child or children have been adopted and all contact has ended (except perhaps for a promise of a once-a-year letter), the incredibly painful process begins, of learning to live with the hole that the child leaves behind. Regardless of whether the birth parent has fought to the end to keep their child, or whether they have come to a level of acceptance that adoption is best for them, the hole is huge and the idea of being able to find a way to live with it often feels like an impossibility.

Alongside the sense of loss, birth parents also carry the heavy burden of shame. Their children will have been removed because they have been judged to have neglected, abused or failed to protect them.

Some – often after the passage of time – will be able to reflect and recognise the ways in which they were unable offer 'good enough' parenting. These mums and dads will feel that they have failed their children and will feel an overt sense of shame. This often makes it difficult for them to allow themselves to grieve. One birth mum, talking about how she missed her two sons and starting to connect with her feelings of loss, abruptly stopped herself and said angrily 'I have no right to feel sorry for myself – I didn't look after them in the way that a mother should!' Our task as therapists is sometimes to help the birth parent to separate out the feelings of shame and the feelings of loss – and to help them to believe and feel that both sets of feelings are valid and are allowed. Only then can they be explored and processed.

Other birth parents will find it harder to understand or agree with the reasons why their children were removed. Some will be adamant that the decision to do so was a wrong one and believe that they were easily capable of parenting their children. But even for these mums and dads, beneath their anger will be some sense of shame: not so overt and not necessarily spoken, but there, nonetheless.

As therapists we learn about loss and we are experienced in working with it. But there is something about being alongside a parent who has lost their child through adoption, as they connect with the sense of emptiness that the child has left behind, that can feel particularly harrowing.

As professionals we use the term 'loss' when we talk about adoption and this is what many birth parents describe feeling. Yet the word is also commonly used as a synonym for death – when a child is adopted they have not died, they are living a life somewhere else and with other people – and here lies some of the complexity of the loss that birth parents experience. One birth father was enraged when he contacted the birth relative counselling service and the person on the end of the phone referred to 'the loss of his child', he screamed 'my daughter is not dead!'

Birth parents certainly experience grief – but this is a particular kind of grief which is different to death and incredibly complex.

Society has a reasonable understanding of what death means and there are accepted ways of how to respond to it. There is normally a ceremony in the form of a funeral – to allow people to come together, to 'say goodbye' and to show support and offer comfort to the deceased's closest family and friends. Often the bereaved talk about a sense of 'closure' once a funeral has taken place. There is no equivalent ceremony in the case of adoption and no closure. One birth mum, Sandra, a year after her three-year-old son had been adopted because of severe neglect, was struggling to cope with him no longer being in her life. She also found it painful to think of him living a new life without her, not knowing what that life was like or how he was getting on. She tearfully whispered to me 'It would have been easier if he had died'.

When a child has died, there is a common language to communicate this and on sharing the fact, the bereaved parent will normally be met with empathy and compassion. Birth parents on the other hand, are left with trying to work out how to respond when people ask if they have children. It's something that people ask all the time: when starting a new job or college course or meeting people for the first time or developing new friendships. Years after an adoption has taken place this question is still likely to come up, leaving the birth parent struggling to know what to say. More than one birth mum has talked to me about her internal struggle when someone asks her such a question: 'do I say "no" and deny my child's existence or do I say "yes" and open myself up to facing questions of where they are?'

Birth parents fear (not unreasonably) that if they share with someone that their children have been adopted they will elicit responses of at worst, harsh judgements and at best pity – either of which will trigger feelings of shame.

During medical appointments birth mums are often confronted with a situation where the practitioner has in front of them medical records indicating that they have had a child and therefore the fear of having to explain that the child has been adopted.

Harriet's four children had been adopted because of her involvement with a series of unsafe men. They had witnessed such things as one of her partners wielding a knife and threatening to slash his wrists, but Harriet, scared herself and unable to properly understand the impact of this on her children, remained in the relationship. During the period of our work together, just under a year after the adoption, she was experiencing pelvic pain and her GP sent her for a gynaecological examination. As a child Harriet had been sexually abused by both her father and then her stepfather and the examination triggered feelings of vulnerability and shame. During the examination, looking at her medical notes (and presumably in an attempt to put her at ease), the nurse commented 'Oh how lovely, you have four children'. Harriet, already feeling vulnerable, felt unable to find a way to indicate that it was a subject that she didn't want to talk about and too ashamed to tell the truth, mumbled 'They are in foster care' to which the nurse replied 'Oh well – I expect you will get them home soon'. Harriet left the appointment in tears.

I often work with birth parents to help them to find ways that they feel comfortable with, to answer the 'do you have children?' question. Louise came up with a phrase 'yes, but I am not lucky enough to have them with me'. She felt as if she would have been betraying them if she had pretended that they didn't exist but that if said assertively enough, this response would set a boundary that would close the conversation down and communicate that she was not prepared to talk anymore about it.

The 'hole' or emptiness left behind when a child is adopted is felt in many ways and on many levels. On a physical level, the sight of the empty cot or bedroom, of the toys that are no longer being played with, or of the coat rack with empty pegs, the silence in the once noisy house, or the empty time previously filled with contacts, meetings with social workers and court dates. On a more sensory level, birth parents talk about missing things such as the smell of the child's hair or the feel of her skin. And on a visceral level, the felt sense of something missing – less tangible but at times overwhelming.

> In the immediate aftermath of her children being adopted Mary talked to me about her days and weeks feeling empty. Up to the point of the adoption, her day-to-day life had felt filled with contact sessions with her children, meetings or phone calls with her social worker or solicitor and court hearings. Even though these things had gradually reduced since her children had been removed she felt as if they had come to an abrupt end once the children were placed with the adopters. There was no longer anything in her diary and nothing of importance to leave the house for. She felt acutely the slow passing of time. With the fight to keep her children over and her last hope gone, this was the point when Mary felt at her most desperate yet. After all of the activity of the past months she felt a sense of abandonment as social services were no longer in her life.

This is often the point when birth parents are referred for counselling. Social workers – once the children have been placed for adoption – are no longer involved in the birth parents' lives but recognise the need for some kind of ongoing support. The opportunity to see a counsellor, even though just for an hour each week, can help birth parents to feel less alone and to ease the sense of abandonment. Mary described our weekly sessions as a life belt – just about keeping her afloat – and without which she believed she would have sunk into despair and drowned.

As time moves on and birth mums and dads become accustomed to the quietness of the house or the empty bedrooms, the felt sense of loss remains, often still as acutely, years and years later.

Living with the pain of the loss can feel unbearable and very often birth parents attempt to ease the pain by filling the hole with other things.

Diane was referred to me just after she had had her Goodbye Contacts and presented as very child-like. She had mild learning difficulties and had been in a relationship which involved domestic violence. We worked together to help her find ways to soothe her feelings and foster a sense of connection to each of her three children even though they were miles away. She learnt that she could find comfort through lying on their beds and hugging and stroking their teddies. Partway through our work she was moved from her family home to a one-bedroom flat. She found this move very difficult - leaving behind the home full of memories of the children - there was no room for the children's beds in her small flat and in the chaos of the move the teddies were lost. Distraught at the loss of her family home that had felt to her like her last connection to her children and unable to find comfort in her flat, she started to go out drinking with a new neighbour. As Diane used the alcohol more and more to attempt to ease the pain, her attendance at counselling started to become irregular. I could see that she was trying to fill the hole with her new friendship and with the alcohol and, though she was able to acknowledge this in our sessions, I could sense her slipping further away and felt unable to reach her. Tragically, after one evening of heavy drinking together her friend died. Diane's reliance on alcohol became worse, she eventually stopped coming to counselling and I didn't hear from her again.

Birth parents find all sorts of ways to try to fill the hole. I have worked with both birth mums and birth dads who have quickly entered into new relationships, but often their lack of any sense of self-worth – reinforced by the shame of having a child adopted – means that they are drawn into abusive or damaging relationships.

With the loss of a child so acute, many birth mums believe that the only way that the hole can ever possibly be filled is by having another baby. As the pregnancy often comes soon after the adoption, the likelihood of the mother having been able to change the circumstances or behaviours that led to the child being removed from her care is very low and so the new baby will in most cases be removed at birth. Professionals often find it difficult to understand why a birth mum would put herself through the pain of having another child removed, sometimes again and again. But the felt sense of loss and the longing for another child – very primal feelings held in the limbic system of the brain – are so powerful that they override any logic or understanding that the mother might have about the likely outcome.

> Julie came to her session the week following a Goodbye Contact which she had been dreading and seemed surprisingly calm and content. During that session and in the weeks that followed I attempted to gently lead her to talk about the Goodbye Contact and to connect with her feelings surrounding the loss of her children. Each time she declined and kept her focus firmly on the future and a new relationship. A few weeks later she told me that on the very same day of the Goodbye Contact she had discovered that she was pregnant! She was happy and excited about having her new child and hopeful for the future. I felt desperately sad for Julie. I knew that it was very unlikely that she would be allowed to keep this baby. The hope of a new child had helped her to avoid making any connection to her sense of loss but I knew that once the baby was born and removed from her, the feelings of grief would come crashing in with yet another lost child on top of the previous ones.

Sometimes, if enough time has passed and a birth parent has been able to change their circumstances, they are allowed to keep a subsequent child.

> Eight years after her two daughters had been adopted Louise fell pregnant again and after assessment in a mother and baby unit was allowed to keep her daughter Mia. Though not wanting in any way to 'replace' her other children, Louise hoped that having her new daughter would in some ways help to ease the pain of the loss. Instead she found the opposite, though watching Mia grow and develop brought her great joy, it also brought acute reminders of what she had missed out on with her other daughters. With every milestone that Mia reached, came fresh pain: she had not been there for when they learnt to ride a bike, for their first days at school or for countless other milestones, big and small.
>
> As she made plans for her first family holiday to the seaside Louise noticed that rather than feeling the expected excitement, she just felt sad – she had never got to take her other daughters on a holiday or to a beach. She realised that she was starting to dread the holiday – fearful that she would be overwhelmed by the sense of loss. We worked with these feelings during our sessions in the lead up to the holiday and she was really able to connect with her grief about missing out on this experience with her other daughters. In the end, she had a lovely holiday with Mia. Rather than try to push the feelings down so as not to spoil the holiday, she had been able to acknowledge the feelings of loss that the holiday had brought up,

to allow them and to take the space to process them. This meant that she was still able to enjoy the experience of her first holiday with Mia and that the sadness, though still present, had not overwhelmed her. Walking on the warm sand, she selected three shells - one for Mia and one each for her other girls.

Millie had been addicted to heroin and her eight-year-old son Lewis had been removed due to neglect. Several years later, now free of drugs and managing her life well, she had been allowed to keep her baby daughter. Delighted, she imagined that being able to bring up her daughter would erase some of the pain of loss which was no longer being masked by the heroin. She came to counselling when her daughter was six. Her awareness of her daughter's needs had made her think about how much she had failed to meet her son's and she was racked with guilt. Dreadful memories were being triggered of her time on heroin. She came to one session distraught. She had been to watch her daughter's school sports day and it had brought back a memory of her son's all those years before. She remembered walking past the school field and noticing that a sports day was taking place. She hadn't realised that morning and had sent Lewis in without his PE kit. A skinny boy, she had been able to pick him out in a borrowed sports top that was far too big, struggling to run in his school shoes where the other kids were wearing trainers. She remembered him spotting her and beckoning her to come and watch with the other parents but instead, feeling ashamed, she had turned and walked away. Telling this story, she could remember the sense of shame but could also now start to understand the awfulness of the experience for Lewis.

Among the horror of her memories from her years of addiction and the consequential neglect of Lewis, Millie was still able to locate small but precious pearls of good memories of her time as his mummy. Waiting for her to arrive for a session one week I applied moisturiser to my hands. When Millie entered the room she immediately recognised the smell of Nivea. This took her to a memory of rubbing the cream into baby Lewis' legs and we took some time together to savour this memory of when for a small but precious moment, she had been able to provide him with the nurturing that she now understood he had needed consistently.

It is clear that having another baby does not bring a 'happy ending' however much birth mums, those around them and sometimes even professionals hope that it might. One birth mum whom I worked with was outraged when a (no doubt well-meaning) social worker said to her after her nine-month-old daughter had been removed for adoption, 'you are still young – you will be able to have other children in the future'. The mother understood though, that no new baby could ever fill the hole inside her that had formed with the loss of her first child.

Sometimes birth parents find healthy ways of attempting to manage the pain and as therapists we can support them to identify people or develop resources that might be helpful. One of my clients found working in a charity shop provided a distraction and gave her a sense of worth, another was taken under the wing of a church organisation which helped her to feel nurtured and valued, and another started a college course which provided her with a sense of hope for a better future.

But even though these things can be helpful in distracting from the pain and in improving self-esteem, the hole left by the adopted child remains.

Ultimately, for a birth parent to be able to live a life as wholly as possible after they have lost their child through adoption, they need to be able to acknowledge, connect with, feel and accept the 'hole' and learn that they can survive it. As therapists our role is to help them in these tasks.

Different birth parents find different and unique ways of connecting with and of expressing their loss.

Exploring the sense of loss with Karen, who experienced feelings in a very physical way, I wondered if she could locate it anywhere in her body. She talked about feeling it very clearly in her heart area. We took some time to explore what this felt like and she gradually formed a picture in her mind of her heart having three holes in it. This was a really meaningful session for her and the next week, she came in with a poem that she had written 'Three holes in my heart' (see p.15). This helped her to transform what had felt like overwhelming, chaotic and confused feelings into something that was easier for her to connect with and to contain. It also allowed her to have more of a sense that she could start to choose when to connect with her loss and when to place it gently and safely in the background.

Harriet, though in her 30s, presented as very childlike and in terms of her emotional development, her age was around ten years old. Thinking conceptually would have been impossible for her so we worked with crafts to find a way for her to connect with her feelings of loss. She was frightened that she would forget things about the children so we made memory boxes out of old shoe boxes. I bought with me a range of wrapping paper and she carefully selected three different designs of paper for each of her three children. She then used sticky letters to add each child's name to their box, taking a long time to carefully pick out the right colour letters for each name. We filled the boxes with photos and different coloured Post-it notes, each with a different memory written on it. Each box had lots of space in it so that she could add new memories as they came to her or birthday cards each year if she chose to. She kept the boxes in her bedroom and knew that she could return to the memories and take them out whenever she wanted.

Each year, the birth mum or dad is faced with having to spend their child's birthday without them. Many decide that they want to mark the day in some way.

Karen's three girls had been adopted seven years ago, but every year on each of their birthdays she baked a cake.

Gary decided during our sessions that he would buy a silver charm bracelet for his daughter Jessica and that each year on her birthday, he would buy a charm for it. His hope was that she would come and find him when she was 18 and that he would give her the bracelet and that she would then know that he had thought about her on her birthday each year. We both knew that there was no guarantee that she would contact him but I could see that it would give him a ritual each year in the absence of sharing Jessica's birthday celebrations with her. It would also be a way of him feeling a sense of connection with her on each of her birthdays.

Diane had mild learning difficulties and presented as vey childlike. In the week's leading up to her daughter Emma's third birthday, the first one since she had been adopted, Diane talked about dreading the day and feeling at a loss as to know what to do. She wanted to mark it in some way but the idea of doing something just felt too overwhelming for her. She had a counselling session booked with me on the date of Emma's birthday. During the session she talked about her memories of her previous two birthdays and I asked what she would have done for her daughter's birthday if she had still been with her. She didn't hesitate - a party tea with cakes and biscuits.

I wondered if she would like us to do something together, in the session to mark the date. She was really keen on the idea and looked to me for a suggestion. So taking her idea of a party tea I suggested that with our cups of tea, we could share a Kit-Kat (which I knew to be her favourite chocolate bar as I had checked it out in preparation the previous week). So we sat together eating Kit-Kats, enjoying the flavour of the chocolate and the sensation of it melting in our mouths and had our own 'party tea.' Afterwards I asked if she would like us to sing 'Happy Birthday' to Emma, which delighted her so we held hands and we sung. She cried as we sung the words 'Happy Birthday dear Emma'. She had been able to celebrate her daughter's birthday, to share the occasion with someone and also to feel the sadness of not being with her.

In most cases birth parents are not allowed to send birthday cards to their children and often bring to counselling sessions their feelings of sadness, frustration and anger about this. It is often difficult for them to understand 'what the harm could be' in sending a birthday card and feels to them like just another reminder of the Local Authority holding all of the power. If I feel like it is going to be helpful, I remind mums that even though a decision has been made that they are no longer allowed to parent their child, it does not mean that they are no longer a mummy. And it follows then, that even though they are not allowed to send a birthday card, no one can tell them that they can't buy one. I work with the energy in their anger to help them to develop some sense of agency. We sometimes talk together about what kind of card they would like to choose. Many then go out and buy a card which they then put aside in a memory box or ask the Local Authority to put on their child's file. Rather than feeling powerless and defeated, the act of buying the card can leave them with a sense of empowerment. They have been able to express and channel their anger in a productive way rather than act out in an aggressive or self destructive way. And on top of that, if their child does get in touch as an adult, they will be able to see that they were remembered on their birthdays.

Christmas too is a difficult time. As Christmas approached Karen talked about her feelings about it and fantasised about what it would be like for her daughters this year. The following week she came in with this poem.

It's Christmas time.

My beautiful girls

I will miss you so much.

Today my heart ached

with a physical pain.

I have my baby girl

Mary Jane – four years old,

but she doesn't replace you

my darling girls.

Nothing will ever replace you.

This year I realised you'll

be grown up enough

to do the tree yourselves.

My four girls together,

that would be my dream come true.

Instead, your Daddy and little sister

and I your Mummy

do the tree.

We put decorations on the tree

that we had when you were tiny babies.

They go up every year.

Decorations that I'd brought each year:

one for each of you.

Just wanted and needed you to know

that you're never far from my thoughts.

From our thoughts.

My beautiful precious girls

my love for you has never dimmed or died.

Nor will it ever be so.

So Happy Christmas

my beautiful girls.

I love you all so very much...

As your little sister would say

'To the moon and stars and back again'.

For any parent, the loss of a child will leave an enormous hole which will remain with them forever. For parents who have had their children forcibly removed for adoption that hole is still there for the rest of their lives but so much more complex to live with. In addition to the loss, birth parents have to find a way to live with both the judgements of others and their own harsh self-judgement and sense of shame. Furthermore, they can only wonder and imagine what kind of judgements their own children will make about them.

Birth parents also have the added pain of knowing that their children are living a life with another family – often one that they know very little or nothing about. With this comes the knowledge that the child is experiencing all of the things that make up a life and that they are not there to share them with them.

Different parents will find different ways to live with the hole that is left behind when their child is adopted. Some will find ways of acknowledging and connecting with the hole and giving themselves the best chance of finding a way to live as complete a life as possible, with it there. Others will just find it too difficult to connect with and will carry it with them without being able to separate it out from who they are.

Our role as therapists is to hold on to our own awareness of the hole that has been left within each birth mum or dad (with its enormity and complexity) even when they can't, to invite them to find a way of connecting with it that is meaningful for each of them, and to recognise and respect when they can't.

Chapter 4

Engagement, Flexibility and Pre-counselling

Joanne Alper and Patricia Downing

I don't know how I will survive these days
existing in a hurt filled haze!

Birth parents who lose their children to adoption, in many cases, have had exceptionally challenging early lives themselves that often result in them struggling with a range of significant social and emotional difficulties. These difficulties are often compounded by ongoing trauma in adult life as the result of involvement in abusive and domestically violent relationships. All of this is commonly the foundation on which they then have to try and comprehend the pain and confusion associated with having their children removed and placed for adoption. Many parents have little understanding as to why their children have been removed, despite this being explained on multiple occasions. They can struggle to see the whole picture from their child's perspective, instead often being caught up in their own emotional turmoil. For many birth parents, the idea of counselling, even at a time of extreme emotional distress, is likely to feel completely alien. Many parents probably would have grown up being unable to talk about their feelings, or have their feelings validated. The idea of talking to someone is unlikely to be associated with feeling supported or comforted.

The chaos and fragility in both their lives and their minds can be overwhelming. It's understandable that many parents would want to avoid the pain of talking and thinking about their feelings, when they are feeling completely raw and exposed. It's not then surprising, that this vulnerable and emotionally fragile group of people would require a more flexible and sensitive approach to therapeutic service provision.

Another barrier for many birth parents is their difficulty trusting professionals when they themselves have just come out of adversarial court proceedings with their Local Authority. Whether that professional is a counsellor or a social worker, we are often perceived as being under the same umbrella, to many parents we are all part of the 'Authorities'. Having considered all this, it is actually truly amazing that so many birth parents have accessed our counselling service. They have been able to take that first really difficult, painful and often frightening step towards their own healing.

Pre-counselling and pending service

Research in 2010 highlighted the need for flexibility in birth parent counselling provision. The research stated that 'Birth relatives need for support varied in relation to different stages of the adoption process' (Neil et al., 2010). In recognition of this need for flexibility and of the changing needs of parents at different times during their child's adoption, Adoptionplus developed what it refers to as its pending service.

Parents don't get a 'one time only' chance for support. It's not a 'use it or lose it' approach, it's much more flexible than that. Parents are informed as soon as adoption is being considered as an option for their child, that they have a legal right to independent counselling support just for them. Our service administrator contacts them and explains all about the service, answering any questions they may have. They then have a choice about whether they would like to take up the offer of counselling at that time. Some parents say yes, others understandably say no. These parents are then asked whether they would like us to phone them back in three months' time to see if then might be a better time for them. The majority of parents who turn down counselling during that first phone call, agree that they would like us to phone them back in a few months. They clearly don't feel ready for counselling at that time, but value the opportunity to consider it again at a later date. It's not unusual for us to do this three-month call back three or four times over a year, if that's what the parents are wanting. Some parents take up counselling as a result of this flexible call-back approach, others appear to just value us calling them when we say we will and check how they are. Although a percentage may never take up formal counselling, a number of people do appear to get some emotional benefit from knowing that we are thinking of them and contacting them when we say we will.

We believe that this flexible approach is helpful in a number of ways. It allows people to consider over time, the option of counselling and reflect on it as an intervention that could be helpful to them. Additionally, as we phone back when we say will, it also helps build the trust relationship they have with our service. People get the message from our actions that we can be trusted to do what we say we are going to do. Lastly and also very importantly, the warm, non-critical friendly approach of the service administrator assists in modelling the warm and non-shaming approach our counsellors take when working with parents. This approach is taken during phone conversations and in the content of letters that are sent. All communications with birth parents are an opportunity to show them that the service and the people who work here, respect how hard this is for them and will do our best to be sensitive to their feelings.

Letters - ensuring they are not a lost opportunity

All mental health services need to correspond with their clients. They need to confirm appointments, as well as obtain and send information. However, time and consideration is not usually put into thinking about the language used, or the impact of these letters on their service users. Many letters can feel punitive if they are about missed appointments. However, with a little time and care, these letters could be opportunities to connect with their service users and portray a therapeutic message of empathy and compassion. It doesn't necessarily need to cost service providers any more money, however the benefits could be considerable. Sometimes it's the small things that make all the difference and a non-shaming and compassionate letter, when people are going through a tough time, can really help people access the service they need for their own emotional health.

> Angela had her first child at 18 and went on to have eight children in total. None of them lived with her having been removed due to concerns related to severe neglect. Angela herself had experienced an abusive childhood involving sexual abuse, violence and neglect.
>
> Despite informing us that she wished to take up the offer of counselling, Angela didn't attend the first couple of appointments or answer her phone when we called. As a result we wrote to her saying that as she had missed appointments we wondered whether now might not be the best time for

her to have counselling. We suggested that we contact her again in three months to check if she might feel ready for counselling then.

This non-shaming, accepting and gentle approach enabled Angela to contact us and take up the offer of counselling. In all our correspondence with Angela we were letting her know that we were keeping the door open for her, that we respected her feelings and that we were providing her with an element of choice and control. There was no blame placed on the fact that she had not attended, instead the careful use of language portrayed a message of respect for the difficult situation she found herself in and a desire to be helpful when the time was right for her.

Without these messages Angela may not have felt confident enough to take those first tentative steps into therapy.

Trust-building and relationships

Once a parent has accepted the offer of counselling, their allocated counsellor contacts them directly and gently introduces themselves prior to the first appointment. The counsellor also uses this call to check they received the map we sent and know where the venue is and answer any questions they may have. At this point we also ask people if they would like us to send a reminder text message before the appointment to help them remember it. The majority of people take up this offer of additional support, recognising that this may be helpful to them.

This call not only assists with clarifying practical information, it also starts the relationship which in turn can take away some of the initial anxiety for parents, about walking into a room and meeting a complete stranger during the first counselling appointment. Additionally this call is also an opportunity for the counsellor to convey a message of care and interest in their welfare, which may help reduce anxiety and promote feelings of safety. We believe all of these factors are beneficial in supporting parents to access counselling.

A sensitive and flexible approach to engagement in counselling

Derek's daughter had been adopted and he was referred to the service, although was very unsure about attending counselling. He allowed himself to be persuaded by his partner, who felt he needed some help, although he himself clearly felt ambivalent about counselling. When I called to introduce myself and confirm the session, Derek said he actually felt he was okay and didn't really need counselling. He asked if he could leave it for now. The answer was, of course that was fine and that if he changed his mind in the future he would be very welcome to contact us and we would be happy to arrange an appointment for him. There was no criticism in either words or tone. I wanted to show Derek that I completely accepted what he was saying. Following this conversation, we wrote a friendly, non-shaming letter to Derek confirming he would be welcome to contact us in the future.

A couple of months later, Derek called the service and explained that he had changed his mind and now felt ready for counselling. At the first session, Derek was apologetic about not coming before and was really quite ill at ease. I reassured Derek that this was not a problem at all, explaining that many parents need a little time before they feel ready to work with a counsellor. We talked about his mixed feelings about counselling and his anxieties about the process. Following this tentative start, Derek went on to attend counselling on a regular basis for a number of months and reported that he found it an invaluable outlet to help with his painful feelings.

We believe that it's very important to be warm and non-shaming in our communications with parents, whether or not they attend. The approach we take in these early contacts, can support them in overcoming their anxiety to try counselling.

As a child Sarah was sexually abused by her father and suffered the additional trauma associated with her mother having significant mental health difficulties. She left home at 14 and became involved with drugs and prostitution. At the time she was referred to counselling with us she'd had three children removed, was homeless and working as a prostitute. She told us that she wanted to see a counsellor as she wanted her life to be different. We found a counselling venue close to where she was staying and set up the appointments. Sarah confirmed that she knew where it was and that she would be attending. However on the day of the appointment she phoned saying that she couldn't make it. She proceeded to explain to me what was going on for her that day and why she couldn't attend counselling that week. This pattern continued for a number of weeks, with appointments being made, but Sarah cancelling at the last minute, choosing instead to tell me on the phone what was happening and how she felt about it. It was clear that there was something about the idea of face-to-face counselling that was too much for Sarah at that time. I gently raised this with Sarah and we agreed that phone counselling would work better for her. This enabled Sarah to access the counselling support that she wanted, over a number of months, in a way that was manageable for her. It may have been that face-to-face counselling might have been too intense or intimate for Sarah to manage. For whatever reason Sarah needed us to be flexible in how we provided her with the therapeutic support she both needed and wanted.

An accommodating approach: Bending the Frame

Bending the Frame (Eversole, 1997) describes a flexible approach to the therapeutic 'frame' which addresses people's complex and ever-changing circumstances.

Often in more traditional counselling services, if a client does not attend a session and doesn't contact the service, they may either not be eligible for further sessions or it may count towards their session quota. At best, a client may be given the 'benefit of the doubt' for one or two missed sessions. However, because of the complex multiple issues many birth parents have often linked to histories of childhood abuse – rape, addiction, domestic violence – it may be incredibly difficult for many of them to engage in counselling at all. Not only do all these factors contribute to difficulties with trust and relationship building, but they also often result in considerable emotional and practical chaos in people's lives. This can mean that they find it difficult to deal with all the practical details of getting to appointments, as self-organisation can be a real challenge. In addition, financial problems may mean mobile phones are out of credit and bus fares not available. There may also be a plethora of appointments with various agencies (e.g. contact sessions, social security appointments, legal advice), that can mean time management skills are really put to the test.

Alongside practical difficulties that can impact attendance there are also emotional factors that can result in missed appointments. These are often associated with the intensity of the therapeutic work that is taking place and people's need to manage the impact this has on them. Understandably sometimes people need to take a break from the emotional pain associated with processing past trauma, in order that they feel strong enough to carry on and move forward with the therapy. We accept that for many people this is what they need and don't shame or penalise them for choosing the pace they need to follow for their own healing and recovery. This is very personal to each individual, but people who have experienced years of extreme abuse, trauma and loss need us to respect the speed they are able to travel at. They need access to services that enable them to have some control over what they are able to process and when they are able to process it. If we want to provide services that are helpful and effective we need to take these factors on board when considering their design.

Pre-therapy and relationship building

As part of the service, as we previously explained, our counsellors contact birth parents by phone before the first appointment. It's an important part of relationship building and can help to support people to attend that often very difficult and scary first appointment. For some people this phone support from their counsellor is all they can manage initially as they struggle with ambivalence about attending counselling.

Additionally this 'outreach' approach could also be seen as a form of 'pre-therapy'. Prouty (1976, 1990) says pre-therapy is helpful where it is difficult for a client to be in psychological contact with another, for those who have been 'damaged by life experience' or have significant mental health issues. In our experience this pre-therapy approach has been a very helpful way of starting to build a relationship where people may have difficulties trusting others and feel anxious about talking to someone about their feelings. It gives them an opportunity to test out if they feel safe with this other person and if they feel able to share their painful and sometimes frightening emotional world with them.

This telephone support often results in parents feeling comfortable enough to attend a face-to-face counselling appointment. However, for some people the counsellor and parent agree that telephone counselling might be the best intervention for them at that time. Telephone counselling is offered by a number of counselling services around the UK, but it's sometimes considered inappropriate for people with a range of complex needs. In fact, there is not much theory or research on the efficacy of telephone counselling, despite its importance as a means of meeting public needs for support, exampled by services such as Childline and the Samaritans. One of the advantages of telephone counselling is that the person has much more control over how much he or she is known, also as to how long the session will last. Often telephone sessions will be shorter, perhaps 30 minutes or so in length and might therefore feel more manageable. Lester (1974) suggested telephone counselling is a situation which increases the positive transference felt by the caller. The faceless helper is readily perceived as an 'ideal' and can be imagined to be anyone or anything the caller needs or wants. Zhu et al.(1996) felt the anonymity of the telephone enabled clients to be very honest and therefore could speed up the counselling process. Additionally it could be argued that telephone counselling could be perceived as less emotionally intimate, as the birth parent does not have to look at another person as they speak about their feelings. As a number of the birth parents we see have attachment and relationship difficulties, that reduction in intimacy and emotional intensity may make telephone counselling more manageable for some people.

Some people receiving counselling have found that they value the opportunity to switch between phone counselling and face-to-face counselling during specific periods. The flexibility enables them to continue accessing support as their circumstances or emotional fragility changes.

> Tabitha was involved in her daughter's court proceedings when she was referred for counselling. She initially attended regularly and utilised counselling well, talking about and exploring her feelings. However, whenever it came close to a court date she would become extremely anxious. She told us she felt like her skin had been peeled off and that she was unable to leave the house. She clearly still needed emotional support during this time so we suggested telephone counselling. Tabitha took this up and was able to get the support she needed. We interspersed face-to-face counselling with phone counselling when needed so that Tabitha was able to access support even at her most vulnerable times.

A number of parents referred to our service have had a mental health diagnosis of agoraphobia or panic disorder and have found telephone counselling more accessible for them.

> Fiona was diagnosed with agoraphobia and rarely left the home she shared with her very abusive partner. Through telephone counselling over a number of months she began to see there might be a different future for her. At the end of counselling she had booked on to a training course and was starting to feel able to leave the house.

Opening doors and building bridges

The importance of flexibility when working with birth parents extends to 'reaching out' to people when they are struggling to engage. We want to make parents aware that if now's not the right time for them, they can come back. It's not a 'one time only' offer, instead it's an open door and a clear path back to into the service. It is not uncommon for birth parents to start counselling and then stop and then start again. People often feel enormously anxious about the idea of counselling and a service that provide a 'use it or lose it' type approach is going to exclude a large number of people who could greatly benefit from therapeutic support.

Jessica was referred for counselling, as her son had been adopted. Jessica herself had been abused as a child and as a result spent many years in a variety of different foster homes. Initially when she was referred for counselling she attended a few sessions, but understandably found it hard to talk about her feelings. She stopped attending after a couple of sessions. We wrote to her saying that maybe she didn't feel ready for counselling yet, but when she did she could contact us. As always our tone was warm and friendly and non-shaming.

Two years later she contacted us again. At this point she had a second child, Milly, whom she was struggling to bond with and this difficulty was impacting on her parenting. Social services were involved trying to support her and providing a range of services to help Jessica safely parent her daughter. Jessica had just started to attend counselling, when Milly was placed in foster care following child protection concerns. Jessica stopped coming to counselling at the time. However, two months later, after a follow-up phone call from us, she decided she wished to return.

At this point Jessica was finally able to engage in counselling. She continued to regularly attend appointments over the next nine months, finding the sessions a useful emotional support and an opportunity to reflect and understand on what had happened and why it had happened. She started to understand that although she cared deeply for her children, being a parent was problematic for her. She started to understand how her own traumatic childhood was impacting on her as an adult.

Her daughter was placed with Claire, Milly's paternal aunt, and through counselling Jessica was able to see that, given her own difficulties, this was best for her child. Her acceptance and understanding of the situation enabled her to develop a good relationship with Claire and over time enabled her to have supervised contact with Milly. Although she was devastated when the decision was made to grant a Special Guardianship Order to Claire, she was able to focus on maintaining contact with Milly in this new arrangement.

The counselling had been really important to her. Not only did she obtain emotional support during a really stressful and painful period in her life, but she also recognised some of the factors that resulted in her children being removed from her. Additionally, as she started to understand and care for herself more, she was able she was able to make the decision to leave a particularly violent partner.

Jessica clearly benefitted from counselling. She received emotional support during an enormously painful time for her; she was able to maintain a relationship with her daughter which was extremely important to her; and she was able to leave her violent partner. However, without the flexible and non-shaming approach it is questionable as to whether she would have been able to access counselling at all.

Many birth parents value the opportunity to come to counselling when they feel the time is right for them. Whilst others, having received counselling, find it helpful to be able to come back to counselling months or maybe years later. Sometime the break from counselling is planned and parents move into our pending system, allowing them to process some of the work they have done. Either way, many parents value the flexibility of being able to come back.

> Janet originally came to counselling for 18 months. She'd been in an extremely controlling relationship with her partner, who at one point had kept her, in effect, as a prisoner in their home. Their two daughters had been removed due to neglect and to witnessing physical abuse.
>
> Janet first felt ready to access counselling several years after the adoption. She had separated from the girls' father once the children had been adopted and felt desperately guilty that, until that point, she had chosen him over her girls. She was also still suffering the effects of the trauma that she had experienced within the relationship and was feeling high levels of anxiety which were impacting on her ability to function in day-to-day life.

We worked with Janet's sense of guilt and, over time, she was able to better understand how living in a state of constant fear had affected her mental health and cognitive functioning and that at the time this had impacted on her ability to make sound judgements or to understand the impact on her girls. Though the guilt never left her, it felt much less overwhelming and was contained within a growing sense of compassion towards herself.

Counselling also focused on helping her to start to process the trauma and to develop resources that enabled her to feel less frightened in her day-to-day life. By the end of our work she had enough of a sense of safety to be able to start work for the first time in over 10 years.

> Two years later Janet contacted the Birth Relative Counselling Service again. Her eldest daughter Charlotte, who was now 18, had been in touch and wanted a relationship with her. Though Janet was overjoyed, as this was

what she had always hoped for, she was also experiencing some other more confusing feelings. Having experienced counselling as something that had previously been helpful at a difficult time, she approached the service as soon as she noticed that she was struggling.

Just knowing that the service is still there once counselling has ended, being able to turn to it in times of difficulty and then having their need for further support responded to, is something that in itself, many birth relatives report as having therapeutic value.

Having already previously established a good therapeutic relationship with her counsellor, Janet was able to use the sessions well and to work through her current difficulties relatively quickly. We were able to revisit her fantasies, from the years that Charlotte had been living with her adopters, about what it might be like if she got back in touch and to explore how the reality felt different. Because we had previously done some work about holding her boundaries, she was easily able to recognise that 18-year-old Charlotte's behaviour was making it difficult for her to hold onto her boundaries. This realisation then allowed her to find ways to establish boundaries in this new mother-daughter relationship.

With Charlotte back in her life and asking questions about her father, Janet also found that some of the trauma of living in a controlling and physically abusive relationship was being triggered. We re-visited and built on our previous work, to enable her to feel safe - even with the possibility of him reappearing in her life.

Janet had got back in touch with the Birth Relative Counselling service when a new situation had arisen. Other birth parents contact the service again when they feel that they are starting to struggle and feel that they need some kind of a 'top up'.

Grace had come to counselling for a period of around nine months, after her two-year-old son had been adopted. She had felt very low, finding it difficult some days to get out of bed and her self-esteem, which had always been wobbly, had plummeted. The counselling focused on her feelings of loss and on her sense of worthlessness and hopelessness. The therapeutic work helped Grace to identify the external things that made her feel better about herself and also to develop somatic resources that helped her to lift herself out of her depressive state. The counselling came to an agreed end when Grace felt that she was ready to manage on her own.

Six months later, Grace got back in touch. During our work, she had learnt to be mindful of her thoughts and feelings and was therefore able to recognise that she was starting to dip again. She used the sessions to continue the grief work that we had started before. The counsellor reminded her of the things that she had previously identified that had helped her to feel better about herself and so they also practised together the use of the somatic resources that she had previously developed.

Her counsellor was able to help her to review and reflect on how she had felt when she had first come to counselling and she recognised that, even though things had felt difficult recently, they were still so much better than they had been. This really helped her and gave her sense that, despite recent struggles, she was still moving forward. Her counsellor also pointed out that this time, she had been able to notice how she was feeling before she got so low and, recognising this, was able to seek support. She finished the counselling with more belief in herself, with a sense that she would be able to manage on her own and that, if she found that she wasn't managing, she would be able to ask for and take support.

Some birth parents go round this loop several times, knowing that the service is there for them for when they need it and learning that if they ask for support it will be given. Returning to and building on the things that they have found helpful in previous counselling. For many, this is their first experience of having reliable, consistent support, of knowing that if they ask, their needs will be met. It gives them the sense of a safety net – as they face the challenges and difficulties of life without their children – they know that if necessary, there will be someone to catch them before they fall.

Conclusion

From Chapter 2 it's clear that not restricting session numbers, or when in the adoption process someone can access counselling support, is important in promoting engagement. Alongside this, in our experience, flexibility and a non-shaming approach are also key to enabling more birth parents to access the therapeutic support they need. Additionally we believe that it's important to utilise all opportunities available to provide birth parents with key messages of compassion and sensitivity to their feelings.

Resources

Eversole, T. (1997) 'Psychotherapy and Counseling: Bending the Frame', in M. Winiarski (Ed.), *HIV Mental Health for the 21st Century*. New York: NYU Press.

Neil, E. *et al.* (2010) *Helping Birth Families: Services Provision, Cost and Outcomes*. London: BAAF.

Prouty, G. (1976) Pre-therapy: A method of treating pre-expressive psychotic and retarded patients. *Psychotherapy: Theory, Research & Practice*, 13(3), 290–294.

Prouty, G. (1990) Pre-Therapy: A Theoretical Evolution in the Person-centered/Experiential Psychotherapy of Schizophrenia and Retardation, in G. Lietaer, J. Rombauts and R. Van Balen (Ed.), *Client-centered and Experiential Psychotherapy in the Nineties*. Leuven, Belgium: Leuven University Press, pp. 645-658.

Lester, D. (1974) The unique qualities of telephone therapy, *Psychotherapy: Theory, Research & Practice*, 11(3), 219–221.

Zhu, S.H. *et al.* (1996) Telephone counselling for smoking cessation: Effects of single-session and multiple-session interventions. *Journal of Consulting and Clinical Psychology*, 64(1), 201–211

Chapter 5

Working with Birth Fathers

Ian Orr-Campbell

I can be a hot head at times but counselling helps me keep calm and talk about things I have on my mind, about life and my children.

Introduction

Studies examining safeguarding children have frequently found that birth fathers can be ignored as either a positive or negative influence in children's lives (Brandon *et al.*, 2009; Brown *et al.*, 2009; Gordon *et al.*, 2012; Zanoni *et al.*, 2013). It's not uncommon for professionals to feel anxious about working with birth fathers especially if they present as very angry and hostile. However, I would suggest that we need to understand this anger, recognise what lies beneath it and find ways to work through it. Birth fathers are often in considerable emotional pain but can benefit hugely from therapeutic support, if provided in a way that is accessible.

During my work with birth family members, I have observed birth fathers to initially appear more withheld. It's noticeable that they seem to struggle more with trust and feel suspicious of the service and of my motivation as a counsellor. Not only do they seem to feel undervalued in their role as a parent, but are also concerned that I may be planning to report back negative information to social services. Additionally and significantly, many of the men I have worked with appear particularly anxious that I will hold them responsible for their children's removal and placement for adoption. In fact at a deep level, many clearly hold themselves responsible and as a result carry an enormous amount of shame and guilt.

Many men I have worked with, in their early sessions seemed to be quick to anger, quick to be defensive and quick to externalise blame. Placing culpability at the door of the 'authorities', their partner, their ex-friends or anyone else, they clearly want to push responsibility for their difficulties and for the removal of their child as far away from themselves as possible. By externalising blame, they hope somehow to free themselves of overwhelming feelings of shame many carry with them.

As a therapist working with birth fathers in these situations I'm aware how quickly feelings of vulnerability and shame can detonate into explosive anger and rage. In order to work effectively with birth fathers, it's important to accept the anger and manage it during the therapy process.

Underlying much of this anger is the crushing feeling of shame. In those moments, with the use of acceptance and kindness, compassion for the self and for others can be cultivated. Self-compassion develops kindness and this can liberate the person from the traps and constraints of guilt and shame

Working with anger in in the room

Greg was in his 50s and had three children placed for adoption because of his neglectful parenting, as a result of long-term drug and alcohol use. He had most of his teeth missing, was covered in tattoos and had a hostile demeanour. The first few sessions involved Greg moving from anger to disengagement on a regular basis. At our sixth session Greg came in to counselling clearly agitated and angry at the start. He informed me that social security had cut his benefits and he was furious about the situation. I asked him how I could be supportive and he got very angry. He got up and started pacing the room 'What the fuck do you think? You fuck me over, they fuck me over, everyone fucks me over.' I remained sitting and seeing that he was highly agitated I wanted to give him some options to support him with his emotions. I stated that it was clear that today was not a good day and said, 'What are the options? You could do one of three things, you could keep shouting at me and then we will both feel bad, you can go out and have a fag, or we could stop and catch up next week and say that today wasn't a good day for it.' Greg decided to take a break and went out for a cigarette. When he came back in he appeared much calmer. He said, 'Oh I got really pissed off then...sorry bout that'. He then sat down and we started the counselling session. In my work with Greg this became known as a 'fag break'. When we got close to a strong emotion that he was struggling with, I gave him the option to stay and work through it or to take the break. On some occasions when Greg got close to something painful and would say that he was going for a fag break I would ask him, 'And if you didn't have the fag now at this moment, but had one afterwards, what would that be like to stay with those difficult thoughts here now?' Sometimes Greg would carry on with the session and sometimes he felt he needed to have a break.

Whatever option he chose it was always Greg's decision and this element of control contributed to a greater feeling of safety in the therapy sessions. It was only when Greg could feel safe that he could start engaging in the therapeutic process.

Feelings of safety are enormously important when working therapeutically with birth fathers. They need to feel that, not only are they safe, but their feelings are safe and will be held and managed without triggering further shame.

John had a daughter placed for adoption due to concerns with regard to neglect. His partner had a slight learning difficulty and John presented as having anger management problems. John was tall and well built and his size alone could leave some people feeling intimated, although, for the first few sessions he came in and presented like a gentle giant. However, during the third session I asked him a question that inadvertently triggered him into shame. He instantly became very angry and aggressive, leaned forward, stood over me and was swearing at me: 'I'm fucking fed up with people like you asking me all these questions...you can fuck off'. Initially I let him vent for several seconds and then very slowly stood. I wanted him to see that I was not threatening him but was making him aware that I respected my own space and clarifying where the boundaries were. I said to him, 'I can see what I've said has made you feel really angry and I don't mean to make you feel unsafe'. I then moved my chair back slightly, then sat down and he sat down. By doing so I was helping to regulate his feelings and was also modelling how our therapeutic relationship would work together. He then moved his chair away so that he could stretch his legs out...and then we began the work. He had to give himself his own space. He was mirroring what I started, which was to create his own safe space.

Issues of safety for both the parent and the therapist are of central importance when working with people with high levels of anger.

Matt was in his 20s, a birth father to two children and presented with a slight learning difficulty. He had a history of violence and had a conviction for attacking someone with a machete. He had been in care himself as a child and had suffered a history of abuse and trauma. The Adoptionplus counselling service had completed a risk assessment as was standard practice whenever there was a potential risk to the therapist. As a result practical steps had been taken to ensure that the counselling environment was as safe as possible.

During our first few sessions I noticed that Matt would get very anxious. His voice would speed up and he would talk very quickly. Sometimes he was prone to angry outbursts, start shouting, would get up, pace around the room and would ask how much time we had left. I soon realised that 50 minutes was probably too long for Matt and decided to check this out with him. 'Have you got some place to be Matt?' Although he said he did, my feeling was that it was an excuse to get out. However, he did keep coming back to counselling so it was apparent that he did want to be there. During the third session I pointed out to Matt that I had noticed that during the last two sessions he always seemed to be in a rush to leave and wondered with him if these sessions were too long. I asked him how long he thought that they should be? Matt initially suggested 20 minutes, but after discussion we agreed on half an hour. 'Will you tell me, Matt, if half an hour's too long?' I asked him and he replied that he would. Then I said what we'll do is start at 1 o'clock, we will be finished at 1.30. Pointing to the clock in the room. Matt was then able to regulate himself, sometimes for longer than 30 minutes. I would say 'We now have five minutes left' and he would say that he just needed a little longer to finish. I kept to the time agreement but allowed him to go on if he needed to.

Matt came to counselling regularly for five months and was able to talk about his feelings, start to regulate his behaviours and recognise what triggered his anger. It was clear that he not only needed me to help him work out what he could tolerate, but also how to manage his feelings if it got too much. By building in some control for him with regard to length of appointment, Matt felt safe enough to be able to utilise the therapy available to him.

Working with men who have suffered sexual abuse

Dennis had been sexually abused as a child and carried with him an overwhelming amount of both shame and fury as a result. As an adult he had never spoken about it to anyone and carried his pain alone. However the rage he often felt came out towards his partner and his children. As a result both his children were removed for their own safety and placed for adoption. Dennis initially came to therapy to discuss the adoption of his children.

The first few appointments focused, as always, on enabling Dennis to feel safe. Seeing how agitated Dennis was at the beginning, I started by making him a coffee as we talked about football. After a time, I would notice his breath would slow, his eyes would soften and his body seemed less stiff. Then I would suggest we could sit down and start the session.

The therapy initially focused a lot on Dennis's feeling of rage and fury as we together started to unpick and understand his triggers and his coping strategies. The early sessions were characterised by Dennis telling me what he had done and I would accept his feelings non-judgementally. Language played a large part of this, I would attune to the tone of what was said and reflect back. After a while I would gently challenge what was said. 'I accept you think he was a wanker, but in what way?' 'How did he appear to be a "divvy"?' This helped develop his own sense of curiosity about his own reasoning and facilitated him to accept stronger challenges without triggering shame later in the therapy.

During one session about two months into counselling Dennis disclosed that he'd been sexually abused as a young boy. He recounted the details factually with little emotion,and then we sat in silence. Dennis said his parents couldn't protect him, then he said 'I couldn't protect my kids from me'. He began to cry.

Dennis said he felt an overwhelming shame as he linked the pain he realised he caused to his children with the devastating pain he suffered himself as a child. This shame was enormous for him. I reflected on how much pain he was in and acknowledged the enormity of the courage he had shown in telling me.

Over several sessions I gently invited him to start to be curious about his feelings, behaviours and how might his anger be connected with his past. We curiously explored levels of anger, annoyance, frustration, hostility, rage and fury. Dennis, over time, became his own emotional detective, attempting to understand and make sense of his feelings and actions.

Dennis came to counselling for over a year and during that period was able to unpick his actions and his feelings and make more sense of them.

He told us at the end of counselling that he felt lighter, less angry and believed he had more tolerance.

'Caught in the past'

Sam was a big man over six feet tall, dressed as a punk, with several noticeable scars across his face and head. Before meeting him, I was aware that he had a history of violence and had been had been verbally abusive to social workers, solicitors and health workers in the past. I had agreed to see him for an initial session to see if we could work together. Due to his aggressive manner and hostility towards professionals I wasn't sure if he would be able to utilise counselling. I am aware a person's reputation precedes them especially if they shout at and are angry with professionals. I wanted to see if, given the opportunity, Sam would be able to explore the feelings that lay beneath his anger.

In that first session Sam shouted a lot at me; at times he would rise quickly out of the chair at a startling speed. Although remaining alert for my own need for safety I was also aware that when working with men, anger often hides deep sadness and, in order to explore the sadness, I would have to work through the anger. I also had to ensure that Sam felt safe enough with me to allow his most fragile and vulnerable thoughts and feelings to be explored. To enable this to happen I remained calm and would reflect back to him what he had just said; each time he would sit calmly down afterwards. Sam became aware I was listening to him. It is such a simple thing, to sit and actively hear a person, yet due to his focused anger on the listener, this wasn't easy to do.

Sam had two children removed from his care, 15 years ago, when they were three and five years old, due to his drug addiction and neglect. When Sam recounted the details of how the children were removed he would shout and become angry. Sam believed 'Authority' should have supported him in parenting and bringing the children up.

Sam said 'I'm stuck, I get so far and then I go back, no I'm not stuck I'm caught in the past'. Sam began to cry. 'I'm a fucking junky and I don't deserve my kids, but if I was an animal you would put me out my misery. No one should live like this.'

Sam never came to terms with his children being removed. During one session he recalled through streaming tears his final meeting with his children and how at the end he fixed his daughter's car seatbelt. As the car pulled away his oldest daughter looked out of the back window and waved at her daddy and he said he ran up the street after the car.

During another session he told me the children's bedroom had not been changed since they left. Their brush still had their hair on it and the pillows still had the indentation of the children's heads upon them. At one point he decided he was stuck, he was angry with himself, angry with the children and angry with authority. He told me that he took several black bin liners, he put all the children's belongings in them and put them out for the refuse collectors. He said he sat there that night until morning, smoking cannabis and crying. Eventually, early morning he heard the bin truck and the banging of bin lids. As Sam told me this he cried. 'I couldn't do it, this was all I had left. I know it sounds loopy, I felt I was letting them go again.' He ran outside and told the bin men to put the bags down. He gathered them all up and tenderly put the room back to the way it was before.

Sam really struggled to move forward with his life and became fixated on the age his daughters were when they were removed. His long-term drug use complicated things, making it harder for him to have the cognitive ability to process the situation and find a better way to manage his pain. What was very apparent though out the period he came to counselling, was the enormous level of emotional pain he was in. For Sam, counselling was an outlet for this pain, a chance to connect with another human being who had compassion for the situation he was in and for how stuck he felt.

Boundaries, fear and safety

Bill began each session by saying 'I very nearly didn't come today', his voice whispery and quiet and his eyes dark and teary. I would remain quiet and Bill would tell me a calamity or catastrophe he was facing today. Then we would begin. He would tell me about his children and how he missed them, he would hold my eye contact, allowing me to see his anguish and then he would look down and become tearful and then remain quiet for several moments. This silence, this space, defined the beginning of most of our sessions.

Bill was small, thin and at times looked quite frail. He carried a red rucksack each time he attended. The rucksack was box shaped. I found Bill would reach into the bag when he felt very anxious, when he felt disempowered.

On one occasion he reached into the bag and brought out a large snake. Bill stood up and the snake's tail was still in the bag. There are many things that go through a therapist mind during therapy sessions...am I able to see the client's frame of reference? Do I understand what is being said? Are there patterns I may reflect back to the client? I was thinking none of these at this particular moment. Thankfully I like snakes, however it was a shock. I noticed how carefully Bill watched me and my response. I saw the disappointment when he knew I wasn't frightened. I wondered if the snake was a way of empowering Bill and making him feel safer and we explored this during the session. Sometimes Bill brought the snake, sometimes not. If Bill was going to talk about his children, the snake would be with him in its bag.

Bill would sometimes come late; now and again would miss a session without contacting me. He occasionally would ask to change the time, enquiring could he come an hour later. Every so often he would say that he had to leave early. Each time I would calmly, gently and firmly remind Bill of our contract, the day, the time and the duration of the session. I felt part of the work with Bill was to uphold the boundaries of the therapeutic relationship, a simple matter of same time, same day, same room and same counsellor would help Bill to feel emotionally held and to encourage him to trust me. This in part is keeping the safe space safe.

After a while Bill was able to talk about his feelings, his guilt and his shame about not being a good dad. 'I was not there for them...the children'. Bill said his ex-partner could not look after their children due to her drug problem. Bill felt he could not look after the children because of his alcoholism, 'So they were taken and I did nothing'. Bill explained the children were removed due to neglect and placed in foster care. Bill said he had not had contact for some years.

I asked Bill 'What do you want Bill?'. Bill remained quiet, his hand on top of the red bag. Bill said he had stopped drinking and he wanted contact with his children. Every so often I press and I challenge. Sometimes the situation necessitates action, the client is ready to move to another part of themselves. I asked Bill, 'How?'

Bill said he could write a letter to his children. I asked what might be in the letter; this led to a whole new side to Bill, a creative and curious side I had not seen before. He asked me to help him write the letter, which took several sessions. During this period I noticed Bill seemed less frail, his frame had filled out and he looked like he was taking better care of himself. We spent time at the beginning of the session talking, instead of the tearful silence in previous sessions.

Managing the shame monster

Lee drank heavily: he told me each bottle was an occasion. I asked him not to come to counselling drunk, so that he would be able to make sense of what we discussed. He said he would wait until the session had finished and laughed. Lee at times would be adolescent in his jibes at me, he would use swearwords and expletives.

Lee had three things he talked a lot about: his anger at social services, his frustration with his sister whom he lived with and his sadness about the loss of his children. Lee told me that he felt the removal of his children was the loss of his life, saying 'this life I have now is shit. I drink to forget... I can't do it in front of family so I go out.'

Lee told me he would start drinking then go missing from home, eventually after days he would come back to his sister's house. Sometimes he would be brought back by the police. Eventually his sister couldn't take any more. When I first met Lee he mostly slept on the streets.

During one occasion very early on, Lee came to the session inebriated. It was winter and he had several layers on, including two coats and four jumpers. I explained to Lee we could not do counselling if he was drunk, so made him a cup of tea and some toast instead.

As we ate toast and drank tea, Lee removed layers of clothing, until he was standing there looking very thin and gaunt. On his hands he had burnt the initials of his children with cigarettes, whilst on his arms he had tattoos of hearts, barbed wire and his children's names scrolled between the two. Lee's face was a study in deep and angry scars, these were across his eyebrows, nose and cheeks.

As Lee ate he said 'Do you know what I like about you? Fuck all' and chuckled. We talked about music and football. After he finished he shook my hand powerfully, put all his coats on, then left. He missed the next session.

During this time I texted Lee, with a non-shaming message in order to keep the connection: 'Missed you today Lee, hope you're feeling alright, take care of yourself and I'll see you next week'.

When I next saw him he was sober. He asked for a tea. Lee was not raucous that day. He said he had thought a lot about his children lately. Staring at the back of his hand, tracing the burn marks with his eyes. He said last night was cold, he'd slept rough. Lee told me that he had been a 'shit dad', that he got pissed when he should have been there for the kids. He became tearful. Lee said the last thing he does before he goes to sleep every single night is find three of the brightest stars in the night sky. These stars he said were his children; he told me he asks God to take care of them and blows three kisses to the sky wishing them goodnight. He told me, 'I do this every night, it's my way of remembering'.

Over the weeks and months Lee was able to talk about the pain of losing his children. This was not easy for him; initially the pattern seemed to be that if he talked about them one week, he would not attend the next. I would greet Lee warmly and be careful not to make any shaming comment about his non-attendance the previous week.

On one occasion he was clear what he had to do: 'Stay clean, come 'ere, eat properly and stay clean'. I remarked he had said stay clean twice, Lee said 'Well it must be fucking important then' and laughed. This prompted a series of sessions all based on how Lee could remain stable in his life. Lee's life became steadier and in addition to coming to see me he also regularly attended a drugs and alcohol group. In fact, Lee stopped drinking, moved back in with his sister and came to counselling for the next six months. I believe he found therapy to support him in being stable in his day-to-day living. I noticed he was increasingly able to talk about painful thoughts and memories and still come back to counselling the following week. We began to focus on his present moment thoughts and the way they made him feel within his body. By Lee understanding these more, these feelings became less frightening and more manageable. Over time Lee appeared lighter and less weighed down by his pain. He even explored helping out at one of the shelters he had attended.

Lee then met an ex-girlfriend and began a relationship with her. Although initially this seemed positive for Lee, when one of her children started to call him 'Dad', it appears to have triggered Lee into a considerable shame response. His guilt and shame about not parenting his own children came back and overwhelmed him and he reverted to drinking as a way to numb the pain. As he spiralled downwards he stopped coming to counselling. A few months later his sister Kay, came to see me. She told me that Lee had died of an alcohol-related illness. She explained what had happened and told me that before he died, Lee had been talking about coming back to counselling. Unfortunately his years of drinking took its toll on his body before he was able to do this.

Shame can be a destructive monster: whilst in therapy, through talking and being present with his pain, Lee's shame was manageable. When Lee experienced a situation that significantly triggered him, the shame felt overwhelming and his first reaction was to resort to his old strategy of using alcohol to numb the pain. Unfortunately, before he was able take back control again, he died.

Conclusion

A study in 2012 regarding birth fathers concluded that professionals often regard them as 'troubled' and 'troublesome' and as a result they are often marginalised. Additionally, the study reported that, with the exception of a few well motivated fathers, most make comparatively little use of adoption support services

However, my experience has been that if they are presented in the right way, birth fathers are able to benefit from therapeutic support services. Support needs to be provided in a way that minimises shame and is flexible enough to enable men to engage at their own pace. There needs to be recognition that the anger many men can exhibit usually hides overwhelming feelings of shame and sadness.

As a therapist working with birth fathers, my approach has been to work together with men to better understand the connection between the emotions beneath their behaviour and encourage their deeper curiosity about it. By attuning to their emotional needs and working as much as possible with what is presented in the present moment, I aim to support birth fathers finding more helpful ways of managing their pain and by doing so improve their emotional health.

Nearly all the birth fathers I have worked with accepted some responsibility for the chaos and crisis in their lives. However, they needed the time and space to do this work.

By talking, sharing pain and guilt, by exploring what triggers and retriggers behaviours, some birth fathers can begin to enable themselves to live a life that is not caught up in the past; that attempts to lessen the fear in their lives and create a stable, healthier person who has compassion for themselves and those around him.

References

Brandon, M. *et al.* (2009) *Understanding Serious Case Reviews and their Impact: A biennial analysis of serious case reviews 2005–07*. London: Department for Children Schools and Families, Research Report DCSF-RR129.

Brown, L. *et al.* (2009) Manufacturing ghost fathers: The paradox of father presence and absence in child welfare. *Child and family social work*, 14(1), 24–34.

Zanoni, L. *et al.* (2013) Fathers as 'core business' in child welfare practice and research: An interdisciplinary review. *Children and Youth Services Review*, 35(7), 1055–1070.

Chapter 6

'No Quick Fix': The Benefits of Longer Term Counselling for Birth Parents With Complex Histories of Trauma and Abuse: Carrie's Story[1]

Kim S. Golding and Jane Gould

This chapter has been jointly written by Kim and Jane. Jane has shared information about Carrie, a birth mother to whom she provided counselling, who has consented to her story being shared. Kim was not directly involved in this therapeutic work. Her contribution in this chapter has been to consider Carrie's story and counselling experience and to provide some commentary from the perspective of the Dyadic Developmental Psychotherapy (DDP) model and theory. Through this, we jointly explore the importance of longer term counselling when working with birth parents with complex histories of trauma and abuse.

Counselling provides clients with a therapeutic space outside of their day-to-day lives. The way this space is used will depend upon the individual and the needs that led them to seek this support. They will have their own goals and expectations. However, all will need a relationship with the therapist that provides them with unconditional acceptance, empathy and positive regard. This supports them to begin to face areas of pain and conflict in their life. It is hoped that through the

---

1   Jane writes: 'Writing a real story that focuses on such sensitive material is not easy. I wanted to remain true to my client and honour her experiences while protecting her confidentiality as much as is possible. Carrie has been keen for her story to be heard and I am also acutely aware of how, in my telling of that story, there is a potential parallel in terms of her repeated experiences of being disempowered and, of feeling powerless, in countless systems. Carrie and I have talked about the use of her story for the book and that feels like it has gone some way towards enabling her to feel a part of the process.'

counselling process they will be able to make sense of their experience with a greater acceptance for the impact this has had on them. This in turn can lead to increased self-understanding, improved emotional wellbeing and positive changes in how they feel about themselves and the way that they live their lives.

Within the UK's mental health services resources are limited and demand is high. Unsurprisingly many statutory counselling services adopt short-term brief therapy models with a session limit. These can fit well for some clients. However, for people with a history of multiple and complex trauma, counselling is rarely short. Another more flexible and creative approach is required.

In order to make successful use of counselling, clients need to feel safe enough to trust in the therapist. The therapeutic relationship that they build provides them with enough security to tell their story. The counsellor helps the clients to reflect on this story and the impact that this has had on them. Over time the clients come to accept this impact, to revise their sense of who they are because of this experience and to grieve for any losses that they encountered during this life experience.

In this chapter we explore the counselling of birth mothers who have lost their children to adoption through a deeper understanding of Carrie's story. We reflect on how, when a mother has a complex and early history of trauma and abuse, this process will take longer. From their earliest experience these mothers have often lived with relationships which hurt and damage. Their view of self, and ways of relating with others, is formed in the context of this. As they mature, they develop defences, ways of being and relating to help them to survive this hurt. They learn to survive against the odds, and they do not easily abandon this. Learning new ways of relating and using this relationship to face the pain of the past will take time, and require periods of active work, interspersed with time for taking breaks and consolidating the work done so far.

Using Carrie's story, we will illustrate the importance of providing counselling interventions which are both flexible and long term.

Carrie: the beginning

Loud and bombastic, Carrie arrives at her first counselling appointment larger than life in body and voice. Carrie grunts her greeting. She is dressed in well-worn clothes, her nails bitten to the quick, the roots of her hair several inches long. She throws herself onto the small sofa causing it to vibrate. She answers her phone: 'Call me back, I'm somewhere', she says and hangs up. Anger seeps from every pore of Carrie as she begins to talk. 'Fucking social services, bunch of twats, set me up to fail, let me down my whole fucking life. Baby snatchers!' She was coming to see Jane because she'd had three children adopted and yet there was no obvious evidence of grief or sadness.

It can be easy to make rapid judgements in the first meetings with birth mothers. The lack of remorse can be off-putting as anger is vented at everyone else. Therapists need to suspend this judgement, seeking to understand the person in front of them, beyond the prickly exterior they first present.

Within the DDP model, the therapist responds to the client with an attitude of PACE (Hughes, Golding & Hudson, 2018). This attitude conveys unconditional acceptance (A) of the inner experience being presented by the client alongside curiosity (C) about this experience. The understanding that this leads to is conveyed with warmth and empathy (E). Playfulness (P) is also an important element of the relationship that is offered. In this initial meeting it will be important than any playfulness is not experienced as a threat but is communicated as genuine interest in the relationship. Playfulness will increase as the relationship develops.

Carrie, initially angry, then reveals an ocean of tears as Jane's warmth and empathy touch her. Tears and grief in overwhelming abundance flow. Shuddering, heaving sobs.

An initial experience of PACE gives clients like Carrie a rare experience of a relationship that is interested in them and their experience. It is not unusual for this to quickly lead to the expression of vulnerable emotions, a vulnerability that can be frightening to them. Clients may return in following sessions with their defences more securely in place. It may be a while before such vulnerability is revealed again. The therapist will need to be patient. PACE will be her anchor, as she allows the client to tentatively build trust over time and as she accepts the many returns to her more familiar defensive style of relating.

In these early sessions Carrie is able to tell Jane about her recent history of a traumatic and abusive relationship. She tells Jane that she had met her children's dad when she was 14 and moved in with him when she was 15. Carrie describes him as being considerably older than her and a violent man who raped and beat her continuously. She describes being so frightened of him she would urinate, defecate or both when he lost his temper. She would 'freeze' when he became violent, completely immobilised in her fear.

Clients will often talk about some of their experience, and this is a beginning. Some of the detail described, as above, can be very harrowing. This impacts on the therapist who is getting a glimpse of the lived experience of her client. Instead of struggling to have empathy for an angry person who is testing the therapist's tolerance, she can experience empathy and compassion for the great hurt that the client experienced both as a child and an adult. Whilst the client might not be ready to receive this empathy, she will feel safer because of the impact her story is having, and the softening in the therapist as a consequence.

The clients test safety with the therapist by revealing some of their story. For now, vulnerability is hidden as they relate factually what has happened to them, often with little expression of the emotions they would have experienced at the time. The therapist responds with non-judgement, compassion and empathy. Only with time and increased feelings of security will clients allow their therapists to use their acceptance, curiosity and empathy to help them share this experience affectively and reflectively. Within the DDP model this is called the Affective-Reflective (A-R) dialogue. It is a conversation which is more reciprocal. The therapist moves from listening empathically to also leading the client into an exploration of the deeper emotional experience about the events being shared. In order to engage in A-R dialogue the client needs both safety and trust in the therapist as well as the capacity to enter reciprocal relationships. These need to build during the early stages of the counselling.

Building safety whilst understanding Carrie's story

At this beginning stage of the counselling process clients rarely feel safe. They are likely to stay controlling within the relationship, avoiding the reciprocity that is both feared and needed. A client might be able to relate her experience (Reflection). She might struggle to hide her grief associated with this experience (Affect). She will however do both of these by herself, not yet able to let the therapist co-create the narrative of the experience or to co-regulate the emotion being expressed. The conversation (A-R dialogue) cannot develop more deeply until the client is experiencing some safety in her relationship with the therapist. The story is told but not yet explored.

When counselling parents who have experienced their children being removed, and subsequently adopted, safety is made more difficult because this beginning is taking place in the context of complex feelings of current loss and grief. Parents are managing the feelings associated with the loss of their child to adoption. This is a multifaceted and intricate grief process full of shame for losing a child who is still alive and being cared for by others. The client remains in the pain of her current as well as past experience: lost in a shame which prevents her from trusting others to help.

Additionally, there are often multiple losses in their lives which they have not fully grieved. Beliefs about the self and why these things have happened are often negative, leading to a sense of worthlessness. This is a complex cocktail of emotional experience that needs to be painfully explored within the counselling.

The first task is to build safety for the client. Listening non-judgementally to the story that the client tells is a first step.

> Carrie details her life to Jane during their initial sessions. As a baby, her mother had punished her by holding her in scalding water, causing third-degree burns. The medical report she shared stated that there were no splash marks, suggesting that she had frozen in fear as her mother burned her. Carrie was in hospital recovering for many months, having almost died from the extent of her injuries.
>
> The very person hurting Carrie and threatening her life, was the one person who should have been there to protect her and keep her safe. Knowing this about Carrie's early life, we can start to understand that trust is going to be a huge issue for her. The idea of a baby, who had already suffered so much abuse and trauma in her young life that she simply 'froze' as she was being seriously burned, is shocking.

When children experience life-threatening events, and escape is not possible, their nervous systems engage a primitive defence, often described as dissociation. This is a response governed by the dorsal vagal system and is generally seen as a last-ditch attempt to escape by feigning death (Porges, 2017). This is most easy to imagine when thinking about prey and predators. At the point at which the prey can no longer escape, the appearance of death can lead the predator to abandon its catch. Eating animals that are already dead carries risk of disease, the predator seeks elsewhere and the prey lives to see another day. These same dissociative responses are seen in humans in extreme situations, for example freezing or shutting down.

When abuse is frequent, the nervous system becomes organised around the high level of threat. Fight, flight and dissociation are all employed as defences to such threats. Dissociation is the most primitive and the riskiest of these, occurring initially at times of fear without resolution. This is often seen in infants who cannot fight nor flee. Later these same defensive responses, including dissociative behaviours, occur when the post-trauma symptoms are triggered by an event in the present, leading the nervous system to anticipate that danger is current again.

The expectation of danger becomes exaggerated leading to an oversensitive nervous system that employs primitive defences even when actual level of threat is low. The therapist needs to be aware that small signs of danger, an expression on her face, a change in tone of voice, a suggestion that she is unavailable or uninterested can all lead the client to display a range of fight, flight and dissociated behaviours. Therapeutic work comes to an end until safety can be re-established.

The therapist needs to develop a good understanding of the client's nervous system which will guide her in how fast or slow to go and when to return to grounding, stabilising and building safety.

When a client spends a large amount of time in a dissociative state, trauma becomes trapped within her and inaccessible to reflection. For these clients, the counsellor may also need to do more experiential and body-focused work. This aids the building of safety and helps the clients to become able to notice triggers and to develop their own strategies for increasing sense of safety. This work often precedes talking about experience. It is important not to rush this process or to expect too much of the client. A longer counselling period will be needed to avoid these difficulties.

After suffering horrific abuse as a baby within her birth family Carrie then spent many months in hospital having to undergo multiple painful procedures to help heal her wounds. All this she did alone, without the consistent safe, nurturing comfort that should have been provided by a parent. From hospital, Carrie was then moved again, this time into foster care. Her mother chose to relinquish her for adoption. She told social workers that she didn't love her, hadn't wanted her when she found out she was pregnant and had never bonded with her. There was no mother stroking her burgeoning belly with care and pride and singing lullabies to her baby within. There would have been no gentle words of future hopes and dreams. For Carrie's mother, the baby growing inside her was unwanted and unloved. There is little doubt that this mother has her own sad story to tell. Carrie was to find out she was not wanted much later in life but it gives an indication of the level of rejection Carrie would have sensed from being in utero.

Eventually, at the age of four, Carrie moved to live with her adoptive family. This was not an easy adoption. Without therapeutic support, it's perhaps no wonder that her adoptive parents struggled to understand how best to develop a relationship with her and parent her in the way she needed. One can only begin to imagine what the adoptive parents were faced with. They were overjoyed to have a longed-for child in their home and they were ill-prepared for the impact of the trauma this little girl had experienced. The only way that Carrie could function in this world was to be in control of her environment - I am not safe, I do not need you, needing you is dangerous, I must be in control, I can't seek comfort, I can't explore the world.

Jane can only tell the story from Carrie's experience, but she is mindful that the adoptive parents' experience will read very differently. Carrie describes never feeling loved, that another adopted child was the favourite. As she grew older her memories are of being chastised, shouted at constantly, smacked and locked in a cupboard. She felt under continual threat of being taken into care. She never felt she had a secure base.

When relational experiences have been frightening and painful, the comfort of emotional connection and feelings of safety in a relationship do not occur. In the absence of these fear of abandonment is high. The child learns to anticipate that the parents will be psychologically unavailable. Moving from home to home adds physical abandonment to this expectation.

With few opportunities to feel loveable and valued the child grows into an adult who anticipates similar abandonment from anyone in role of caregiver, including the therapist. Some clients are attracted to relationships which offer a false sense of safety, idealising attributes such as strength and power and anticipating these as protective. Some may become victims expecting to be hurt; this validates their belief that they are a bad person and deserve to be punished. Painful though this is it protects the victim from a different pain. If she allows herself to feel worthy of care and nurture, the expected loss of this would be devastating.

Unsurprising then that when she was 14 an abusive older man was able to target the vulnerable Carrie and engage in a violent and destructive relationship with her for many years.

It is likely that Carrie felt that this man understood her and that sex became evidence of his 'love' for her. Carrie would have been desperate to feel a connection with someone, to feel wanted and loved. Her experiences of rejection would have compelled her to seek out someone who could give her what she needed. To be made to feel attractive and interesting, to be important in someone's life, to be prioritised – all of these experiences would have inflamed the embers of her need for a 'mother figure' and the experiences attached to that.

The violence continued during and after the births of her children. Carrie believed her partner wouldn't hurt her if one of her children was in her arms and they became her method of survival. Unknowingly they stopped many a beating for their mother and perhaps even saved her life.

Carrie was able to escape this living hell. It was a usual day in Carrie's life, one that was filled with fear, self-loathing and sadness. Her partner started yet another argument and his anger was quickly fuelled. Rage pouring from him, he raised his fist to hit Carrie. In that moment one of her children threw themselves into her arms. Carrie knew she had to escape. Experiencing her own child putting herself at risk to protect her at the age of three finally enabled her to do what she needed to, knowing her children were being damaged by the violence they were exposed to. This provided Carrie with the motivation to finally leave.

It makes complete sense given Carrie's early life, that she would have difficulties forming healthy relationships as an adult. Her early experiences continued to 'play out' in her adult relationships, the abuse and neglect resulted in her developing a sense of herself as intrinsically bad and other people as unsafe. Carrie found that abusive relationships fitted her sense of self. She had defences in place that helped her to cope with these relationships. She lived her life not needing to trust anyone.

Clients bring their life lessons into the counselling relationship. Sometimes they also bring healthy parts of themselves. The resilience of mothers to escape violence for themselves and their children can perhaps be the kernel of resilience that propels them into the therapy room. The role of the therapist is to discover and nurture the strengths and resilience alongside accepting that other parts of the client are deeply hurting and vulnerable. The client needs time to feel safe enough to reveal all these parts.

Carrie escaped with her children and a few belongings and moved many miles away into a refuge. Over this time Carrie had located her birth mother and resumed some contact. The area she moved to was where her birth mother lived. In her heart she wanted to believe her burns from childhood were an accident and that her mother loved her and wanted her in her life.

Carrie turned to alcohol to help her get through the loneliness and stress of her time in the refuge. Despite her making the choice to leave she experienced this as another abandonment - the act of being alone re-triggering thoughts, feelings and behaviours from the past.

Despite being able to tell Jane this story, Carrie struggled to trust her. She initially related to Jane as she had to all significant adults in her life. She was puzzled when Jane responded differently, persistently meeting her with unconditional positive regard, warmth and empathy whatever Carrie said or did.

Clients will often try to avoid getting pulled into a relationship with the therapist, fearing that this is a trick which will eventually lead to the hurt and/or abandonment that they are used to. They redouble their effort to appear uninterested. They demonstrate their beliefs that they are not loveable. They may be angry, remote, unpleasant as they try and push the therapist into being what they fear she is. Sometimes they are charming: a coercive attempt to ward off the rejection that they have been trying to elicit. Their need for and fear of the relationship moves them between these behaviours. It is only with time that they can start to try out a different way of relating, one which builds on the fledgling safety that they are starting to experience. Longer term counselling allows clients the time to work through this process.

Carrie had developed coping strategies to deal with pain and shame. She used alcohol as a way to numb any pain she felt. However, in her bid to protect herself, Carrie was inadvertently setting up another crisis. She describes the alcohol as taking away the psychological pain of being alone and feeling intrinsically bad and unloveable. Her own distorted thinking resulted in her leaving her children in the care of her abusive birth mother while she went out and got drunk. At this time Carrie was struggling desperately. She was alone and afraid. More than anything she wanted her birth mother to be the perfect mum she'd fantasised about as a little girl growing up. She wanted desperately to have a close and loving relationship with her.

Carrie trusted her mother with her children because it was simply too painful for her to accept her mother could have hurt her the way she did. Alcohol allowed her relief from her inner pain and the capacity to disconnect from the potential danger she was subjecting her children to. She could live in a world that enabled her to be numb and detached and a world in which her pervasive thoughts were blissfully quietened. This came at a great cost however. Her inability to keep her children safe ultimately led to Carrie's children being removed. She had to live with the knowledge that her own behaviours had led to her losing her children.

When a therapist is working with clients who don't trust, this lack of trust can have many layers. Trust in the wrong people and mistrust of those who could be helpful is a common pattern. Trust in alcohol and drugs can seem an attractive alternative when trust in relationships has been misplaced or feels too dangerous. The therapist will be mindful of this complexity when inviting the client to place trust in her. Building trust alongside offering safety becomes the next part of the counselling process.

Trust and building a therapeutic relationship

When Carrie was referred for counselling, she was unable to describe any healthy nurturing relationships that she had experienced in her life. She will need time and patience to discover a new way of being with her counsellor, not hidden behind a wall of defences, but able to reveal the best and worst of herself and discover these are equally acceptable to Jane. Short-term counselling would not allow this process to happen and is unlikely to be helpful for Carrie.

It is widely recognised that trust is important in any therapeutic relationship. However, if a person's past experience of relationships has been abusive, this is likely to result in much greater difficulty in trusting the therapist. Individuals with a childhood history of abuse and trauma will have learnt that people in positions of influence can seriously harm you. They fear a pattern repeating that they have experienced many times before. Trust in the therapeutic relationship is essential if it is to be effective. Any counselling service for birth parents needs a process that provides time to allow trust to develop and grow.

As the clients begin to experience trust in their therapists, they then need further time to start to experience this relationship as different from abusive relationships that they have known. They need time to gently and carefully test out how their most sensitive and vulnerable parts of themselves will be treated by the therapist. Step by tentative step they begin to feel safe enough to use this relationship to explore what has happened to them, to process the trauma associated with this and to develop a different sense of self.

Clients need to know that this time is available. A sense of the sessions being time limited, and uncertainty about how long the counselling will last means that they are unlikely to build trust in their therapists. Already anticipating loss, they will guard against the hurt of this by not opening themselves up to the relationship in the first place. Similarly, typical processes, such as contracting with the client that missed sessions will be deducted from their total number of sessions or stipulating that a number of missed sessions will lead to the counselling being terminated will only serve to reduce trust further. Clients need to test the relationship with the therapist. They need to miss sessions, walk out of sessions, and generally control content and timing before they can settle into a more reciprocal relationship within which they can trust the therapist to have some influence over them.

It is not unusual for lack of trust to be revealed in abusive and insulting behaviours towards their therapist. Clients do their best to drive the therapist away rather than waiting for rejection. During this time the therapist needs to remain steady. She demonstrates that she will keep them both safe, not allowing physical abuse for example, whilst the client is given the time and space she needs to test out whether this relationship is really different. The therapist will maintain her acceptance and empathy for her client even through these most testing of sessions, and especially when providing boundaries for safety. Always the client needs to experience the relationship as central, and acceptance as unconditional.

Working with anger and shame

Carrie was completely detached from her innermost self. She had to be this way to survive in her dangerous world. She had no sense of whom she really was and valued nothing about herself. Living with the pain of this would be far too difficult. Carrie needed defences to help her cope. Her main defence was anger. Anger directed outwards helped her to ignore or deny the complicated feelings that she carried about herself. Her vulnerability was hidden behind a wall of anger.

Defences are unconscious strategies which protect from painful and difficult emotions. They provide some sense of safety in a highly unsafe world. The therapist seeks to help the client to understand these defences, but without pressure to remove them. Stephen Porges names these as 'heroic defences' in recognition of the role they have played in the clients' lives (Porges, 2017). The defences become part of the story that client and therapist are discovering together.

> Carrie is full of anger and rage, motivated by a desire not to feel guilt, to avoid shame and to dissociate from fear and hurt. This defence is used so often that she has little awareness of the vulnerable feelings she is hiding and no awareness of the dynamic driving this anger. Carrie is unable to share her vulnerable feelings because this risks her becoming more vulnerable. She uses her anger to attack others. In this way she avoids her own feelings of hurt and shame. Projection is one of Carrie's forms of defence. This involves her making others responsible for her thoughts and emotions because she cannot bear the feelings of shame or to face her painful emotions. It is easier to be furious with her social worker and blame him for removing her child than to face the pain that she is responsible for her own loss. To accept that is to accept that she is not the loving parent she thought she was, and these feelings are deeply shameful and intolerable.

The therapist is presented with these defences, even as trust is developing. This is a process of discovery and storytelling (Hughes *et al*, 2019). The therapist initially helps the client to tell her story of anger and blame, accepting her need for this. With time she will be able to co-create a different story, one of pain and vulnerability. Typically, the client will oscillate between these as she takes steps towards trusting the therapist with the more vulnerable parts of herself and then retreats back to the safer territory of defence and anger. This cannot be rushed. Developing stories of hope and resilience out of stories of shame, anger and self-blame is the process of counselling parents whose children have been adopted. The path that therapist and client go on will not be straight but will have many winding lanes and dead ends. Ending counselling partway along the path would potentially leave the client in shame and despair.

Shame is another emotion that commonly leads to the need for defences, especially when a child had no adult regulating the early experiences of shame. Without regulation shame grows and becomes toxic to the sense of self. The child is likely to develop her identity around this shameful experience. She develops a sense of being a worthless child.

This shame follows the child into adulthood, impacting on adult relationships. She will be reluctant to trust the relationship with the therapist because she is afraid to be known and to be discovered as worthless. Often the client fears further abandonment and hurt. Instead of trusting others she is likely to have developed defences against the negative feelings associated with shame. Like a shield against the shame she has learnt that anger, minimising, blaming others and lying about herself keeps the shame at bay. This becomes her wall behind which her vulnerable self hides (Golding & Hughes, 2012).

Stuck in shame, clients with these difficulties get lost in their sense of badness and struggle to look outwards and understand the impact they are having on others. They can't experience guilt and remorse because the shame is all-consuming (Tangney & Dearing, 2002). Others become frustrated and angry with their apparent indifference to the hurt they are inflicting. Defences can be life-saving but over time they erode the possibilities to form healthy relationships.

Carrie has a propensity to default to shame, based on her early experiences, and the loss of her children would have caused her shame in abundance – it feels like her fault they'd been taken away. Her defence is extreme anger. If she could blame social care and how they'd let her down her entire life, then she could avoid connecting to her intense and intolerable shame.

A birth parent stuck in shame is not able to reflect on their actions. They are more likely to become angry and aggressive, blame others and potentially misuse drugs and alcohol: anything to avoid the pain of the shame. Understandably, being stuck in shame is going to make any kind of therapeutic relationship more difficult, and an understanding of this is key if counselling is going to have a positive impact.

Developing relationships: attachment and intersubjectivity

At the centre of the counselling relationship, especially emphasised in the DDP model, is intersubjectivity (Hughes *et al*, 2019). The development of some trust and safety opens the way for the client to experience a different type of relationship.

Short-term counselling does not allow time for gently easing a traumatised client into this relationship. The therapist relies on the client having some past healthy relationship experience to draw upon. The focus is on providing the client with a therapeutic space within which they can explore the issues that have brought them into counselling. The client who has some belief in her essential goodness and anticipates that others will value her can use the counselling relationship in this way.

Clients with trauma histories do not carry these beliefs. They have mistrust rather than trust in others and have learnt to control relationships as a way of avoiding reciprocal, trusting interactions. Time is therefore needed to help them to discover a different way of relating, one which has intersubjectivity as central.

To understand intersubjectivity, it is first necessary to reflect on attachment development. Attachment security offers the secure base needed for the child to begin to explore the world of self, other and experiences. This exploration occurs within the attachment relationships. The child develops understanding through the shared meanings that these relationships provide. This is the process of intersubjectivity. The capacity to enter into an intersubjective relationship is influenced by the attachment experience of the child.

As Bowlby helped us to understand, a child is born with an innate instinct to attach to her caregivers (Bowlby, 1982). When the child is responded to with sensitivity, attunement and empathy, she experiences her needs being understood and met. The child experiences safety and can develop a secure attachment. The parents become a secure base from which she can explore her world.

Central to this exploration is the social-emotional world of relationships. Humans are a social species and learning about self is embedded in the experience of others. To give an example, a child picks up an ornament and accidentally drops and breaks it. The parent is initially upset and berates the child for his clumsiness. The child experiences himself as clumsy because this is how the parent experiences him. The parent regrets her harsh words and now offers comfort to the child. She communicates that although the child was clumsy on this occasion he is not a clumsy child. She values and loves him and communicates this through her desire to help him to feel better, a process called relationship repair. Now the child experiences himself differently. He can get things wrong and be clumsy on occasion, but this does not define him. He is loveable and of value to others. The child's developing sense of self comes out of many interactions with his parents.

This process of learning is best described as intersubjectivity. We develop the meanings of our social-emotional world through sharing experiences with others. (Hughes *et al.*, 2019, p.16)

Intersubjectivity describes a reciprocal process of influence. One person is open to the influence of the other and will influence the other in turn. The child is influenced by the parent. In the example above, the child is upset because he has been clumsy and Mum is cross with him. The mother is influenced by the child's upset. She comforts him and communicates that she wants him to be more careful but she will always love him.

Within counselling, the client who can enter into an intersubjective relationship will discover different meanings about self, other and experiences she has had because of this reciprocal influence.

When a child's attachment experience is one of insensitivity, mis-attunement and lack of empathy, insecure attachment will develop. These attachments are even more troubled when the attachment figure is also the source of pain and terror. Children adapt their attachment patterns to this parenting experience, either avoiding emotional connection to keep the parents close (avoidant attachment), or using this connection coercively to ensure parents remain attending to them (ambivalent attachment). When the parent who should be the haven of safety is the source of pain, adaptation becomes harder (Main & Solomon, 1986). The child develops what researchers describe as a disorganised attachment (Solomon & George, 1999). The disorganisation of behaviour (freezing, approach and avoidance at the same time, hand-flapping) indicates that the child cannot feel safe. As the child grows older an organisation does happen, centred around control. The child uses extremes of the avoidant and ambivalent patterns to ensure that they remain in control of the relationship, an illusion of safety.

The abused child has negative intersubjective experiences with his parents. The child who breaks the ornament experiences the parent as angry with him because he is a 'useless, no good kid'. There is no repair. The child experiences himself as useless, and not loveable. This child will have many such interactions all communicating that he is not of value to the parent, he is not wanted, perhaps that he is wicked and evil. The parent's influence on him signals a lack of safety. The child learns to control the relationship rather than be open to this influence.

The type of abusive experience we have been exploring has been described as developmental trauma (Cook *et al.*, 2005). The traumatised child struggles to trust even when they are now safe and being cared for by alternative parents. This leads to complicated attachment behaviours. These children are likely to display all of the avoidant, ambivalent and disorganised patterns of relating in their relationships with their adoptive parents. They will also resist intersubjective connections.

Without support and understanding the adoptive parents can get drawn into responding in a way which perpetuates the attachment patterns, responding to avoidance with some relief, the coercive ambivalent behaviours with frustration, dissociation with puzzlement and unwittingly signalling a lack of safety to the child that perpetuates the disorganised attachment style. Parents can feel hurt or disappointed when the child resists their attempts to soothe and nurture. This experience can lead them to withdraw from the intersubjective as well. Without specialised parenting the trauma will not heal.

With no other template for relationships these children grow up and bring these same patterns of attachment and intersubjective relating into their adult relationships.

> Carrie was scared of everybody around her but she was unaware of this. She had learned to adapt her behaviour in response to this fear: demonstrating aggression when feeling under threat from 'professionals' and submission around violent men. She is likely to demonstrate similar behaviours towards her children, and this combined with the domestic violence surrounding them would be frightening for them. Having not experienced loving, nurturing relationships herself, Carrie is unlikely to know how to nurture her children, despite her evident love for them.

These patterns of relating are also brought into the counselling relationship. This relationship is based on intersubjective experiencing, but clients like Carrie can only come to this slowly. Reciprocity will often be absent during the early work with birth parents, especially when there is past trauma. Intersubjective connection is actively feared. Being open to the influence of the other, in this case the therapist, would require more vulnerability than the parents feel safe to display. The therapist needs to stay open to the client through a lot of testing and controlling behaviours.

It is difficult for these clients to trust that the therapist is being genuine. They suspect that her warm, empathic style is being used to manipulate them, to trick them in some way. When no manipulation is forthcoming, they are likely to be puzzled. They may fear that the therapist does not know them well enough. They expect that the therapist will inevitably discover what they believe is true: that they are worthless and not worth bothering with. They anticipate that as this becomes known the therapist will change towards them. Hurt and pain will surely follow.

Carrie finds it hard to believe she is worthy of Jane's attention and is suspicious about her intentions. She is quick to withdraw, criticise and respond aggressively the moment she feels under threat in any way. A simple question or a moment of humour can easily be misconstrued, and Carrie's barriers will be erected immediately.

Carrie has no faith in anyone around her, always on her guard and looking out for evidence to prove she is right not to trust. She is hyper-vigilant to trust breaches in her relationship with Jane.

Managing defensiveness and remaining open and engaged

The therapist needs to remain open and engaged towards her clients through all the different, and sometimes difficult behaviours that these clients display. Being open and engaged invites the other into an intersubjective connection. Social-emotional experience then become safe rather than dangerous and counselling can begin to jointly explore current and past experiences.

Through fear clients initially resist these invitations, remaining defensive or moving quickly back to this if they begin to feel vulnerable. It is physiologically difficult to maintain an open and engaged stance towards someone who is being defensive (Porges, 2017). The counsellor is pulled towards defence too. This might be expressed as frustration, or even a premature attempt to reassure the client ('you are a good person') or to try and offer some solutions ('why don't you try…'). The client is not in a state to hear these and will view any signs of the counsellor's frustration as more evidence that she is not safe.

The therapist needs to remain open and engaged towards the client. She needs to notice their inevitable moments of defensive responding. Once noticed the therapist focuses on returning to the open and engaged state and actively repairs the relationship with the client. For example, she might acknowledge that her intervention has not been helpful and let her client know that the relationship is important and valued and she will keep protecting it. At times the therapist needs to notice things in her clients' behaviour that persistently trigger her own defensive responses. She will reflect upon this in her own supervision. This strengthens her resilience, allowing her to maintain an open and engaged stance towards her client even at these tricky times.

Over time this continuously signals signs of safety which the client slowly begins to believe in. Trust and security develop, and the client becomes more open to the intersubjective experiences being offered. The client is learning a new way of relating.

It is only when she feels safe enough to be open to intersubjective connections that the client will be ready to use the counselling sessions to reflect on her most difficult of experiences. As she reveals her emotional experience, she is highly vulnerable. As the therapist keeps her safe in this vulnerability, the intersubjective influence of the stories they are sharing together can begin to change the way the client makes sense of these. Only then can her sense of self be revised, and her intense self-blame reduce. There will be many times when this becomes too difficult and the client reverts to the more familiar defensive behaviours. The therapist patiently waits until the client is ready to move back into the more difficult territory of vulnerability.

Building enough safety and offering intersubjective experiences to a client who distrusts these takes time. Clients are learning a new way of relating to another person. They are also learning to trust that their vulnerability will be safe with the therapist. In turn, the therapist responds on a moment-to-moment basis to what her client needs. She judges when the client is ready to go deeper into the emotional significance of the experience she is exploring. She provides emotional co-regulation to support her in doing this. She decides when to return to lighter topics to offer a break from the intensity of this. She notices when her client is no longer feeling safe enough to continue and works to re-establish safety for her. Always the relationship is first. If this is attended to then the process of counselling will flourish.

This can be very difficult to do when the counselling is time-limited. The pressure to complete the counselling process before sessions run out can override good intentions to attend to the relationship between therapist and client. A client with complex needs requires time to build trust, safety and relationship before processing of experience can occur. A rush to move to the 'business' end of the counselling process effectively slows down progress. A longer term contract for counselling can remove the pressure from the therapist to achieve results. This allows her to stay mindful to the needs of the client.

Creating new narratives together

Once the client starts to trust the therapist, and is beginning to tolerate intersubjective connections, the process of co-creating the narrative can begin. Story discovery and the retelling of this story is a central part of DDP. It is important that the counsellor listens and understands the client's experience from the client's perspective. This means sitting with painful beliefs and fears that the client holds. Only when the client feels heard and understood will she be open to reflection, and the possibility of an alternative narrative can be considered.

> Carrie starts to share her most painful feelings. She makes it clear that she hates herself; feeling completely to blame for her difficulties in being able to parent her children. Sometimes the intensity of the pain is too much, and she will rage to avoid her feelings of intense shame. Carrie feels to blame, and it is important for Jane to be alongside her in this process. Ultimately it is Carrie's truth and she and Jane will need to find a way that Carrie can go on living with the knowledge that the children have been lost because of behaviours that she engaged in. Understanding that some of these behaviours might have stemmed out of the influence of her early abuse history will come later. For now, Carrie needs to experience Jane's compassion for her, even when her darkest feelings about herself are revealed. Carrie voices that it would be easier to die. How can she live with this level of self-blame and self-loathing?
>
> Carrie cries so much in these weeks; her pain seems to seep from every pore. She hates herself for not leaving her abusive partner more quickly. Confusedly she also loathes herself for leaving him, believing if she'd stayed, her children would still be with her. She despises herself for her drinking. It is vital that Carrie experiences an adult relationship where she can be fully herself - warts and all - and her feelings can be completely accepted.

Experiencing radical acceptance can be a very freeing process. Clients learn that, whilst they do not feel acceptable to themselves, they are acceptable to the therapist. Their feelings and beliefs about themselves are not right nor are they wrong, this is just how they feel.

As her acceptance and empathy are tolerated, the therapist can move on to being curious about why the client feels this way. Now the past is revisited, this time with a deeper emotional impact. The client can begin to explore what had been impossible to think about. Maybe there are reasons for how she feels about herself, and whilst this does not condone her subsequent behaviours, it does make them more explicable. A new narrative is being created, a story of understanding and compassion which holds out hope that maybe she isn't the bad person she believes. Maybe she is a good person who makes mistakes. The path from shame to guilt is being laid, and with it the opportunity to make some amends. However, there is a sting in the tail of this narrative.

Carrie has to confront her feelings and beliefs about her mother. Jane helps Carrie to think about what her mother did. Carrie is likely to have grown up to believe she was at fault for her mother's rejection. Children are by their very nature egocentric and unable to see a situation from another's perspective. It is therefore difficult for a small child to come to a view of the mother as bad. This also maintains a loyalty to parents by understanding the pain and hurt as being somehow her fault. The parent is idealised, and the self is denigrated. As Carrie looked at this anew, she comes to understand a new potential truth, that maybe her mother had done wrong to her. This means losing the idealised image of her mother that she has held for so long, and with it the belief that one day her mother could be the person that Carrie needs, accepting and loving her without conditions. Carrie has to grieve the loss of the mother she has been yearning for.

Some time into the work Carrie decides she will access her social care records. Jane supports Carrie to articulate her questions about her past. This process finally enables Carrie to accept the reality: her mother had seriously harmed her and then gave her away. Rage and grief consume her. Carrie is in contact with her birth mother at this time and her questions are answered with lies, her grief met with hostility. She has lost the hope of having a loving birth mother; however, with time grows a grudging acceptance about her birth mother and then, increasingly, a relinquishing of dreams and fantasies about her being or becoming the perfect mother.

Within the DDP model the quality of the conversations with clients are important. In exploring what happened and the emotional impact of this therapist and client discover the story together, a process of co-creation. This is intersubjective. The therapist is influenced by the client, experiencing compassion for the difficult experiences being described. The client in turn is influenced by the therapist's experience of the story. The affective element allows the emotions associated with events to be explored together. This helps to co-regulate the emotional experience of the client as she moves into memories of the event and engages in reflection about these. The client re-experiences the event through the counsellor's mind without the traumatic meanings which would have been given by the perpetrator. Together the client and counsellor discover new meanings of events. Feelings of shame and terror reduce in this shared exploration and a new story emerges which becomes integrated into a more coherent narrative.

During this part of the counselling process grief can be intense, and without the therapist's support the client can retreat to the familiar patterns of self-blame and idealisation that she has lived with for so long. This feels like solid ground whilst ahead of her the world appears unstable.

> These are the times when the work becomes overwhelming for Carrie and her repeating patterns become too shameful for her to reveal. At these times she leaves the counselling, convincing herself that she is okay and no longer needs support. Her world then comes crashing in again and she returns. The return is never a failure - the success is in her ability to accept and ask for help and support again.

The therapist accepts retreat as well as progress without judgement but with understanding and compassion. Only from this place can client and therapist begin to be curious together about these repetitive patterns and begin to develop an understanding of them. Only then will the client be ready to take firm steps forward – steps through her grief and loss and towards a new narrative, one of compassion for self and the resilience that comes from improved emotional wellbeing.

> Jane's relationship with Carrie is key and, in some ways, it is really that simple. Carrie experiences, for the first time, a relationship which, despite her best attempts at sabotage, remains unconditional, unfaltering, attuned, intersubjective and compassionate. This approach is fundamental in the healing process for Carrie. Jane is fortunate to be part of a service that recognises the difficulties clients can have in engaging with therapeutic work. She is able to continue to offer Carrie a space when other services may have withdrawn.

The consistent offering of the counselling space, and the acceptance when it isn't used, gives clients an experience they often haven't had before. The longer term nature of the counselling is essential to give client and therapist the time and space that they need to travel a long road together, allowing time for trust, safety, relationship, understanding and new narratives.

So what happened with Carrie?

> As time went on, the therapeutic work continued to impact on Carrie. She made more eye contact, smiled, teased Jane and talked much more about her feelings rather than facts. She started taking care of herself, getting her nails and hair done, and generally looking after herself better.

Carrie smiled a lot more in between her tears and laughed a lot too. She couldn't quite forgive herself for the loss of her children, but she was now compassionate towards herself and accepting of who she was and why she had made the choices that she had. Carrie decided to have a break from the counselling, knowing that she could re-refer herself in the future if she felt she needed to.

In repeatedly offering unconditional acceptance of feelings, and opportunities for intersubjective connections, clients are eventually able to receive these. They begin to accept and understand themselves in new ways. They can take care of themselves better, emotional well being improves and the client becomes more able to consider the future.

Five months later Jane receives a call to tell her that Carrie has re-referred herself to the service. A different Carrie enters the therapy room this time around. Having the break allows Jane to see how Carrie had grown more into her own skin. There is much less defensiveness, she smiles warmly and hugs Jane. She confides that she is pregnant again. She is determined to keep this baby and is back to continue the work.

Carrie gets to keep her baby but this is no fairytale ending. Her life continues to be chaotic. She will continue to need support perhaps throughout her life.

Longer term work has many benefits for parents like Carrie. Being able to understand and grieve for their past and the hopes they have brought with them; being able to take responsibility for the loss of their children and to let go of them; being able to rebuild their life and to focus on their future. These are all significant.

The grief never leaves Carrie but she is able to see a future and she is able to smile again.

Conclusion

Mothers who have lost their children to adoption not uncommonly have a complex history of trauma and abuse in childhood and adulthood. Short-term work does not provide the time needed to develop safety with the therapist and to trust in the therapeutic relationship. It does not allow time to go at the client's own pace. She needs to find new ways of relating, overcoming fear of intersubjective, reciprocal interactions;

trusting in the co-regulation of the therapist; and eventually joining with the therapist to co-create the stories of her life; past, present and potential future. The mothers learn to reflect on their past experiences in order to make sense of their current world.

Short-term work does not allow breaks when things become too overwhelming and opportunities to return when the client feels able.

> Within a brief, six-session model, the client is only just beginning to get to know the counsellor. It took those initial sessions for Carrie to be able to relax and sit back in her seat, rather than to be perched on the edge, ready for a quick getaway should her feelings overwhelm her. It took significantly longer for her to be able to reveal her true self. With time Carrie was able to reveal the innermost parts of herself that she had hidden away through fear. When these vulnerable parts were accepted without judgement, she began to learn that every aspect of herself is important and of value, leading to the dissipation of painful and shameful thoughts and feelings. Carrie needed time and support to be able to face her future without fear. She will need continuing support at those inevitable times when her history comes back to haunt her again.

References

Bowlby, J. (1982) *Attachment and Loss, Vol. 1 Attachment.* London: Hogarth Press; New York: Basic Books. (Original work published 1969.)

Cook, A. *et al.* (2005) *Complex Trauma in Children and Adolescents.* Psychiatric Annals, 35:5, 390–398.

Golding, K.S. & Hughes, D.A. (2012) *Creating Loving Attachments. Parenting with PACE to Nurture Confidence and Security in the Troubled Child.* London: Jessica Kingsley Publishers.

Hughes, D.A., Golding, K.S. & Hudson, J. (2019) *Healing Relational Trauma with Attachment-Focused Interventions: Dyadic Developmental Psychotherapy with Children and Families.* New York: W.W. Norton & Co, Inc.

Main, M. and Solomon, J. (1986) 'Discovery of a New, Insecure Disorganized/Disorientated Attachment Pattern.' In T. B. Brazelton and M. Yogman (Eds), *Affective Development in Infancy.* Norwood, NJ: Ablex. 95–124.

Porges, S.W. (2017) *The Pocket Guide to the Polyvagal Theory. The Transformative Power of Feeling Safe.* New York: W.W. Norton & Co.

Solomon, J. & George, C. (1999) *Attachment Disorganization.* New York: Guilford Press.

Tangney, J. & Dearing, R. (2002) *Shame and Guilt.* New York: Guilford Press.

Chapter 7

'Contact' from the Birth Parents' Perspective

Carole Green

When they see a smile on my face,

I let them think its true...

While a silent scream escapes my heart,

Because I'm far from you.

Historically there was a belief that closed adoptions were in the best interests of both the child and the birth parents. A relinquishing mother in 1968 (the year in which adoptions in the UK reached their peak of 24,831) would have been advised to 'forget' that her baby had existed and 'move on with her life'. Similarly, the adoptive parents would have been advised to parent the child exactly as if she were their biological child and to minimise discussion of adoption. It was uncommon for birth parents and adopters to ever meet. The information given to birth mothers about the adopting family and the adopters about the birth mother was often scant, if not inaccurate. The child's adoption was viewed as an event, a moment in time, of little relevance once it had taken place. For both the mother and the adopted child it was necessary to keep the adoption secret as a protection against the stigma of the child's illegitimate birth. As a consequence, contact between the child and their birth family after adoption was exceptionally rare. The need for openness of conversation about adoption within the adoptive family was not recognised and it was not uncommon that children were not even told they had been adopted.

In more recent years, we have come to a new understanding of the lifelong impact of adoption on the child, particularly the impact of closed adoption on the child's identity development and the issue of unresolved loss for birth parents. Furthermore, children are being adopted beyond infancy and we have developed a better understanding of their need to make sense of their history and to be able to process their loss. This has led to more open arrangements in adoption, with birth parents often having the opportunity to meet adoptive parents or exchange letters with them. Face-to-face contact between parents and children after adoption however remains rare.

A recent overview of the findings of research into birth family contact in adoption has discussed the benefits and challenges of contact for adopted children with their birth parents. This review highlights that well-managed contact can help everyone involved in a range of ways. For birth parents particular benefits are around getting information about the child's progress and the positive impact of this on feelings of loss. Birth parents also value the opportunity to make a positive contribution to their child's life through providing information and reassurance that they have not been forgotten. Although contact is frequently highly valued by birth parents, it can be a mixed or challenging experience as parents struggle with the boundaries around contact, the complexity of their feelings about the adoption and the reality that their child is now growing up in another family. It is important for the child and adoptive parents that birth parents are able to respond positively to letters or meetings and, because of the emotional and practical complexities of contact, many parents may need help with this, particularly in the early days of the child's adoption.

Much has been written about contact, but this chapter seeks to offer an insight into the emotions related to the contact experience from the birth parents' perspective. The areas covered are those that have been raised directly by birth parents during counselling.

The Goodbye Contact

It's hard, perhaps impossible, to imagine what it must be like for a mother or a father to have to say goodbye to their child, at best until they are 18 and at worse forever. As a therapist and also a mother, as

I hear my client's experiences of their 'Goodbye Contacts', I often find that I am asking myself the question: 'Could I do it?'

As they walk away from their son or daughter following the Goodbye Contact all that they are left with is a fragile hope, but no guarantee, that they will see their child again when they have grown into an adult. And with this comes all kinds of fears: Will they want to see me? Will they be able to find me? Will they be angry with me? Will they forgive me? Will they remember me? How will I explain to them why I couldn't keep them with me?

And in the meantime, there are the intervening years in which the child will grow, develop, start school, change schools, make friends, fall out with friends, visit new places, laugh, cry, be embarrassed, find new interests, go to their school prom and all of the hundreds of experiences and milestones big and small that they will no longer get to be a part of.

All or some of this may be going on for the birth parent as they approach their final hour or so with their child for the Goodbye Contact.

And yet we know how important it is to make the experience of the Goodbye Contact as positive and healthy as possible for the child or children. As they prepare the birth parents, this will necessarily be the focus for the professionals involved. We place huge expectations on the birth parents to be able to manage their feelings and remain regulated in order to make the experience a good one for the child. And for professionals involved to be able to prioritise the experience of the child or children whilst remaining sensitive and supportive of the birth parents is an enormous and complex challenge.

One element of the Goodbye Contact is the marking of the occasion: recognising and acknowledging its significance by making it something special. In this way it can also provide the opportunity for a positive memory to look back on.

Often birth parents will come up with their own creative ways to experience and represent their 'goodbye' during that final contact session and social workers will normally have a range of suggestions when needed, whether that be creating something together with their child that they can each take away, sharing food, taking photographs, exchanging gifts, reading a favourite story, playing with a familiar toy or just talking together. What is important is that the birth parents find a way that is right for them and for their child.

Attending a Goodbye Contact is incredibly difficult for birth parents or other birth relatives and understandably for some it is just too difficult and they never make it. Reflecting on the experience over 10 years later Louise told me, with tears rolling down her cheeks 'It's the worst thing anyone could ever be expected to do. I don't think it's right for parents to not go to final contact, but I can understand it.'

Louise had two girls adopted at the ages of three and one as a result of concerns regarding physical abuse, her youngest daughter being removed from her in the hospital at just a few days old. Eight years later she fell pregnant again and, determined to 'do the right thing', she got straight in touch with social services to let them know. They were involved throughout the pregnancy and, after assessment in a mother and baby unit, Louise was allowed to keep her third daughter Mia. As a child Louise had been sexually abused by her father and, in order to survive the experience, had learnt to disconnect from her feelings. This 'survival strategy' had stayed with her as an adult and after her two daughters had been adopted she was able, to some degree, to shut down the most painful of her feelings about the experience of having her children removed.

With Mia now two years old, Louise was finding that being a mum again was triggering all kinds of difficult feelings around the loss of her two older girls and that her learnt ability to disassociate from her feelings was starting to fail her. She was anxious that this was affecting her ability to be the good mother to Mia that she desperately wanted to be and this was her motivation to come to therapy. Most of our work was focused on helping Louise to gently and safely connect with her feelings about the loss of her two daughters and on Louise's relentless judgements of herself as a 'bad mother'.

Though she hadn't spoken about it for over 10 years, when Louise shared her memories of her Goodbye Contact with me, it felt as if it had happened only yesterday. The intensity of the pain and anguish had not diminished over time and in the retelling of it Louise could easily connect with those feelings. She described it as being like 'in a fish bowl' with note-taking by the contact centre staff that felt 'constant and intense'. She said 'It felt like they were expecting us to run off with the children, they were hypervigilant, jumpy every time we moved'.

When asked what she would want to say to professionals involved in Goodbye Contacts, her key messages were: 'Don't ever say "we know how you feel". You don't! It makes a terrible situation much worse. And, don't say anything unless we ask you to: it is the last time we get to see our children as children - don't intrude on it.'

The experience of talking about her Goodbye Contact awoke really strong feelings of anger for Louise which we were able to work with. Having her voice heard, was validating and empowering for her. She was also able to make useful links between the scrutiny and judgement that she felt from the professionals during contact and the pressure that she put herself under now to be a 'perfect mother' to Mia.

The feeling that Louise had – that the staff in the contact centre were watching for her to run off with the children – was not an unreasonable one. Many birth parents talk about the impulse to make an escape with their child at the Goodbye Contact.

> As the day for his Goodbye Contact with his daughter Jessica drew closer Gary started having fantasies about taking his daughter and making a run for it. He started to think about how he could do it and where he could escape to. He realised of course that it wasn't a realistic option but that didn't stop him imagining it.
>
> As a child Gary had witnessed regular domestic violence between his parents. He recounted to me a story of sitting in the passenger seat of his father's car aged four or five, looking up at his father who was driving to the hospital with a knife blade still stuck in his bleeding left arm. As a young adult Gary's only model for conflict was to either avoid it or to fight physically. He got into relationships where he would become violent towards his partners and had served a custodial sentence. Shortly after Jessica was born, Gary's relationship with her mother broke down and he moved out. At 18 months, Jessica was removed from her mother by social services due to neglect. Gary was living with his own mother, who did not want him to bring Jessica to live with them and told him that she thought that he wouldn't be able to manage being a single dad and should let the adoption go ahead. So without the support of his mother or the confidence to disagree with her and without any belief in his own ability to be a father, Gary decided not to fight the adoption.
>
> Gary didn't plan to live out his fantasies about running away with Jessica during the Goodbye Contact but even so as he carried her around the room the urge to make a run for it with her still in his arms was almost overwhelming. As it turned out, with his history of violence, social services had arranged for a police officer to be present, which would have made it impossible.
>
> When Gary came to therapy a year or so later, he still wondered if the police officer had not been present, whether he would have run. During therapy he was able to imagine playing out his fantasy. His urge to run was accepted without judgement and he started to be able to see it as the natural instinct of a father. The fact that he did not act on this instinct was also noted. However, the positive therapeutic element of this situation for

Gary was that he was able to reframe his feelings at the time in in a way that felt less shaming for him.

The Goodbye Contact is obviously really important for the child. It will be their last experience of spending time with their birth mother or father before moving on to a new family. Birth parents are encouraged to make the experience as healthy as possible for the child and to convey positive and helpful messages.

> Jenny came into the therapy service just one week before her Goodbye Contact, she was briefed by the social worker about making it a good experience for her children.
>
> Jenny described being 'told' she would have to hold her tears and emotions in for the benefit of her children and felt her children would look back on the memory and wonder why Mummy hadn't seemed upset. She felt that they would grow up believing that she didn't care and was glad to see them go. She felt the process was unnatural and that she wasn't able to say or do the things that were in her heart.

The question and confusion of whether it is better to 'show emotions' or not during Goodbye Contact is a recurrent one. In this case the social worker's presumably well-intentioned advice about the impact of Jenny becoming emotionally overwhelmed in front of the children had been received by Jenny as being 'told not to cry'. The result was that the experience had felt unnatural for Jenny and so in all likelihood confusing for her children.

In order to have been better able meet her children's needs in the Goodbye Contact, Jenny needed to first have the experience of having her own needs met. Unfortunately Jenny only had one session of therapy prior to the Goodbye Contact. In an ideal world, she would have had somewhat longer. This would have given her the therapeutic space to explore her own thoughts and feelings about it. Her therapist would have been able to support her to mindfully experience and process her feelings during sessions and develop resources to feel the emotions without becoming overwhelmed. Some psych-education would have helped her to understand the impact on her children of her becoming dysregulated.

Perhaps, if this had been able to happen Jenny would have had the understanding and the resources to be more connected to her own emotions and experience during the Goodbye Contact without becoming dysregulated. If she had cried, her tears would not have felt overwhelming to her and would therefore be much less likely to be overwhelming for the children. Ideally her children would have been able to see that Mummy was sad to be saying goodbye to them but that those feelings were tolerable (for her and therefore for them).

The question should perhaps not be whether to show emotions or not, often translated as 'to cry or not', but more about emotional regulation. Social workers who have a good understanding of this are better placed to support birth parents to make the unavoidably painful experience of the Goodbye Contact as healthy as possible.

Social workers will of course bring their own history and experiences with them and this will inevitably impact on their own ability to tolerate painful emotions in others.

> Selina was determined that she would use the Goodbye Contact with her five-year-old son Alfie, to make him feel as positive as possible about being adopted.
>
> As a child Selina's mother had been an alcoholic and her behaviour towards Selina had been inconsistent. At times she had ignored and neglected her, at others she had bullied and picked on her and at others she had shown love and warmth. As a child Selina reached out for the 'loving Mummy' but felt confused, rejected and frightened when her mother ignored or turned on her. At the age of 14 Selina had been sexually abused by her maternal uncle and from that point on moved back and forth between home and living with various friends.
>
> Not long after the abuse she got into a violent relationship which she had been in and out of since. Selina had left her partner nine times since Alfie was born but always returned to him. Following a stillbirth Selina decided to put Alfie into foster care for a short period as she was aware that she was not coping. Psychiatric reports showed that Selina had a personality disorder. She had used a variety of unhealthy coping mechanisms in the past in attempts to try and regulate her feelings and these included disordered eating, alcohol, drugs and self-harm.
>
> Selina had conflicting feelings about the plan made by social services for Alfie to be adopted. On one hand she felt relieved that he would finally be safe from her violent partner, but on the other she was also distraught to be losing her son, especially after the loss of her second child at birth. In our therapy sessions leading up to her Goodbye Contact Selina talked about these conflicting feelings.
>
> Many birth parents experience these kinds of conflicting feelings: recognition that they have not been able to cope and that their child will have a better life with adopters but devastated by the resulting loss.

During the contact Selina felt well-supported by the social workers and willingly engaged in the activities that they had organised for her and her son. They painted each other's hands and feet and made prints for each other to keep.

Selina described to me the way in which she had been able to put her feelings of grief and loss to one side for the two hours that she had spent with Alfie and to stay connected to her thoughts and feelings about adoption being the best option for him. She had told him that she loved him, that she would miss him, but that she was pleased that he was going to have a new Mummy who would be able to keep him safe and who would also love him. She told him that she knew that he loved her and that it would be fine for him to love his new Mummy too.

Selina told me that she felt that, as his mother, this was the last thing that she could do for him - sending him off with her blessing was her final gift to him. I felt a little in awe of Selina and of this ultimate, unselfish act that she was able to do for her son.

Her own mother had not been able to keep her safe but she had finally been able to ensure that her son would be safe. We worked with this 'good mother' bit of her and she was able to connect with feelings of pride in herself. Up until this point in her life, she had not had much to feel proud about and had certainly not been proud of herself as a mother.

Selina's therapy was punctuated by spells in a mental health unit as she wrestled with her feelings of loss and tried to manage without her normal coping mechanisms. But amongst all of the confusion in her mind, there were moments of real clarity where she was able to hold onto this sense that she had been able to keep her son safe and this remained with her throughout.

For Selina, the involvement from the professionals during the Goodbye Contact had felt supportive and helpful. This was in contrast with Louise (mentioned earlier), who had experienced their involvement as 'intrusive'. This demonstrates the importance of taking the time to work with the birth parents to try to understand their own particular needs in terms of support for the Goodbye Contact.

Gail was another birth mum who worked really hard to keep her own distress out of the Goodbye Contact with her six-year-old son Richard, so as not to upset him.

Gail was adopted herself but the adoption broke down when she was 12 years old when it came to light that she had been physically and sexually abused in the adoptive family home. Gail spent the remainder of her childhood moving from one foster placement to another, never feeling safe and frequently running away.

Richard was removed from her when he was a year old due to neglect and because of Gail's involvement with a risky partner. Richard was then placed with an aunt and uncle under a Special Guardianship Order and Gail continued to have a significant level of ongoing contact with him. Sadly, this placement then broke down when he was four years old and he was placed in foster care.

The foster carers subsequently decided to adopt Richard when he was six years old. Gail recognised that she was not in a position to parent her son and the foster carers met his needs well and he was happy living with them. Therefore, she supported the plan for him to remain there; however, she wanted to have ongoing contact and did not want him to be adopted. The court decided to grant an Adoption Order with no ongoing contact.

Gail asked her social worker to support her by transporting her to the Goodbye Contact and meeting with her afterwards.

At the end of contact, Gail managed to hold herself together and not cry as Richard said goodbye to her and went home with his future adopters. Gail walked out of the building and as she rounded the corner out of sight of the workers, she began to cry uncontrollable tears. Her grief was such that she fell to the ground in emotional distress. Her social worker saw her and supported her with her distress.

The support of her social worker had been invaluable to Gail both in terms of practical support (with transport, for example) and emotional support. She had her own social worker because she herself had been adopted. In most cases, birth parents do not have social worker support either before or after the contact. Very often there is also no support from friends or family and the birth mum or dad is left completely on their own.

One birth mother had no support and no transport and after leaving her Goodbye Contact in tears had to wait on her own at a bus stop to catch a bus for the 40-minute journey home alone.

History is often being repeated: these birth parents who very often as children did not get their own practical or emotional needs met are once again facing a difficult experience and painful emotions alone.

Sometimes a Goodbye Contact takes place when the child is still a baby. Sophie had had to say goodbye to her son Harry when he was just six months old.

Sophie had had a very disrupted early life. Aged four when her parents separated, she was sent to live with her grandmother with no explanation. She had no contact with either of her parents until her grandmother died when she was 13 and was sent back to live with her estranged mother where she felt completely unwanted.

When Sophie was 15 she fell pregnant. Her mother was furious and told her that she could not keep the baby. Sophie felt as if all the plans and arrangements for her baby had been made between her mother and the social worker and that she had not been allowed to take part in them. She said that she gave birth to a son whom she just caught a glimpse of before he was taken away by the midwives.

Six months later and despite her mother's objections, social workers arranged for Sophie to come and meet Harry and to say goodbye before he went to live with his adopters. Sophie arrived terrified; she felt awkward and uncomfortable and didn't know what to do with this baby boy that was her son. The foster carer was kind and gentle and led Sophie to a comfortable armchair where she carefully placed a sleepy Harry in her arms.

Some 12 years later as she sat with me in a counselling room, Sophie talked about how easy and natural it had felt to hold her son. She could remember exactly how it had felt: the weight of him in her arms and the warmth of his skin. When she told me the story it felt as if everything else around her had faded into the background for that hour that she sat holding Harry. She couldn't take her eyes off of him and recalled to me every last detail of the red and blue outfit that he had been wearing. This Goodbye Contact didn't need to include any words or symbolic activities but an environment was provided that allowed Sophie to experience it fully.

With a childhood history of sudden endings without 'goodbyes' and without any support, Sophie had been able to experience something very different with her son.

It was a precious memory that Sophie had kept to herself for all those years. By sharing it with me, once again, in an environment that was safe and supportive, Sophie was able to re-experience the wonderful feelings of that time with Harry. In later sessions we used this connection that she had felt with Harry as a baby to help her to connect with him through the writing of her contact letter.

Sometimes, understandably, attending the Goodbye Contact just feels too difficult for a birth parent and they don't make it.

Even birth parents who have managed to attend regular contacts up to that point sometimes just can't bear to face the final goodbye.

Samantha's son Oliver was removed at birth. The social worker who supervised the penultimate contact with Oliver talks about a 'lovely contact': photographs were taken and Samantha held Oliver and fed him. She arranged to be there to support Samantha for the Goodbye Contact, which had been arranged for the following week. However, Samantha never made it to the final contact. The social worker said that she believed that the thought of attending a final contact was just too painful for Samantha and she just couldn't face it.

Meeting the adopters

Sometimes birth parents are given the opportunity to meet their child's adoptive parents once their child has been placed with them. The prospect of this can evoke all kinds of emotions for the birth parents (and no doubt for the adopters too).

At 16, Jasmine met her partner who was a heroin user and was controlling and violent towards her. A year later she gave birth to a baby boy - Karl. Jasmine felt unable to leave her partner and so at four months old Karl was removed from the couple for adoption. Jasmine attended contact regularly and once adoptive parents had been identified, was offered a meeting with them.

She was highly anxious about this: still in many ways a child herself, the idea of meeting the strangers who had been judged to be more capable of looking after her son than she was filled her with fear. However, she was also desperate to meet them and to see for herself the people who would be bringing up Karl. I helped her to think about what she wanted to say to the adopters and to prepare a list of questions that she had for them. She knew that she was at risk of becoming overwhelmed with anxiety and forgetting what she wanted to say during the meeting so felt that having things written down would mean that she wouldn't walk away from the meeting upset with herself for wasting the opportunity.

Like Jasmine, many birth mums and dads find it useful to use their counselling sessions to think about the kind of things that they want to tell their childs adopters about themselves and their child and to think about the questions that they want to ask. Sometimes, they have no idea what they want to say, or where to start and so some gentle prompting or suggestions can help them to think about what is important to them. All kinds of questions come up, simple things like: 'do you have any pets?' or 'what kind of music to you like?' and bigger questions like, 'how will you discipline them if they are naughty?' or 'will you stay at home and be a full-time mum or are you working full-time?'

> In our session, which was scheduled a few days before the meeting was due to take place, Jasmine was starting to feel quite terrified. She was aware that there would be the two adoptive parents and just one of her. She was worried that she might feel like a child in the room with two adults and as the adults in her life had been unsafe and inconsistent, this was evoking feelings of fear. However, she still desperately wanted to meet them. I suggested to her that she consider asking someone she trusted to go with her for support and she said that she thought that would be helpful.
>
> The following week, she told me how the meeting had gone. She had seen her dad the night before and had asked him to come with her, which he had agreed to do. However, he had been drinking and the next day had forgotten all about it and didn't turn up so Jasmine ended up going alone. But despite this, she had felt that the meeting had gone well and had been able to ask all of her prepared questions. Meeting the adopters had reassured her and she felt that Karl would be loved and well looked after.

Not all birth parents feel so positively about meeting the adopters.

> Initially Debbie had no desire to meet her children's adoptive parents. She said that she felt like they were stealing her children and 'hated' them for it. She was able to explore these feelings in her counselling sessions and with that exploration came awareness that this couple weren't responsible for the loss of her children. As a result of this she told the social worker that she did want to meet her children's adoptive parents. Debbie told me that the meeting had gone well. She described being reassured that they were a nice couple and that everything they said had helped her to realise her children would be well looked after. She said that the couple had told her that they hadn't been able to conceive and Debbie felt that her children would be very special to them.

> Diane was acutely aware of the judgement of others. She had mild learning difficulties and had been in a relationship which involved domestic violence. She wanted to meet the couple who would be adopting two of her children but was fearful of what they might think of her for not being able to protect them. In the event, the meeting went well. Diane had really liked the adoptive parents, who had been very gentle and friendly towards her. Their attitude towards her made her feel that her children would be well cared for.

A few week later she received an unexpected letter from the couple. They wrote about how much they had liked her, how much she clearly loved her children and how glad they were to have met her. Diane was delighted that she had been liked: she felt that they hadn't judged her harshly and knew that in the years to follow, they would only ever speak well of her to her children. This felt really important to her.

Letter contact

Very often, for birth parents who have a letterbox scheme in place, their year somehow becomes shaped around that month when the letter is due. As the date approaches, a mix of emotions rise: excitement at the prospect of longed-for news of their children, dread of possible bad news and nearly always, as each day passes, a gradually increasing, nagging fear that this year – there will be no letter.

Gary's daughter Jessica had been adopted three years before we started working together and her adopters had written him letters each year. As the date approached for his next letter he talked through the routine that he had developed for when each one arrived: when the letter came, he would leave it on the table in his hallway for a few days before he opened it. Each letter felt so precious to him, that he really wanted to savour the moment when he first read it. But he also knew that reading news of his beautiful daughter would bring up all sorts of emotions for him - and that frightened him. Gary, coming himself from a family where the only 'acceptable' emotion was anger, had never learnt that it was safe to feel anything other than that and feared that he would either be unbearably sad or overwhelmed by anger, which would lead to violent behaviour. The letter for him, felt both precious and frightening and he knew that he needed to work up his courage to open it.

His partner was used to his routine and knew that he would open it when he was ready and that once it was opened, he needed to be left alone for a few days to cope with the emotional fall-out that might ensue.

As we looked together, at Gary's routine he realised that having it in place was a way of helping himself to feel safe and in control. When he finally opened the letter he was able to enjoy reading about Jessica and told me, bursting with pride and pleasure, that she was a happy and popular girl at school and had learnt to ride her bike without stabilisers.

Harriet's young son and baby daughter had been adopted nine months ago. She knew nothing at all about the people who had adopted her children or about how the children were getting on. In our sessions together, she talked about being frantic with worry about the children - she still felt all of the natural worries that any mother might feel when her children are away from her - but without any way of getting reassurance that might ease her worries.

Eventually two lovely letters came - the adopters had written one about each child. Harriet brought them to our session and we read them slowly together, savouring each new piece of information about her children. I could see her visibly start to release, to let go of the worry and tension that she had been holding and to let the soothing and reassuring words wash over her. The love and tenderness that the adopters had for her children showed through in their words, as did their gentleness and generosity towards Harriet. Harriet had delayed development and saw things in a very simple, childlike way. She often talked about the 'bad people' in the world (sexually abused by both her father and her stepfather as a child, her world had been dominated by 'bad people') and as we finished reading the letters she concluded with relief 'my children are with good people.'

Kevin read that his daughter had been on holiday abroad and reflected 'I would never have been able to give her those kinds of opportunities'. I could tell that despite a hint of sadness he experienced huge pleasure at the thought of her enjoying such adventures and felt gratitude towards her adopters.

Birth mums and dads often read through the letters searching for things that will help them to sustain a sense of connection to their child. Looking for ways in which their child is like them (as most of us who are parents do) they will tell me: 'He's just like me – I used to like swimming when I was a kid' or 'fish and chips is my favourite food too!' Sophie was delighted to hear that her son, adopted as a baby and now 12 years old, loved to play on his Xbox and told me that after our session she was going to get hers out again.

Once a birth parent has received a letter, it is their turn to write back. For some this is relatively straightforward and with good support from a Local Authority letterbox coordinator and a clear set of guidelines they are able to write a letter that they are comfortable with. For others, it can be a much more difficult process.

Sarah felt a huge responsibility to make sure that the letters that she wrote for each of her two daughters were 'just right'. Knowing that she would not get the opportunity for another year and so wanting to convey everything that she possibly could and also aware that the letters might be really important to her girls, she agonised over what to write. She felt caught in a trap of heavy responsibility and guilt. She couldn't bear the idea that she would not do herself justice in the letters or not give the girls what they needed from her, but as each day passed the was acutely aware that her daughters would have another day without a letter.

She laboured for weeks, never quite happy with what she had written, putting them aside and returning to them several times before finally sending them four months after they were due - four months in which the girls may have been waiting and perhaps wondering whether their birth mum didn't care enough to write. Nothing could have been further from the truth.

Some birth mums or dads just feel at a loss as to where to start or what to put in their letter. Some find the thought of approaching a letterbox coordinator who they only see once a year too difficult. This is where, if we have been working with them for some time and we have developed a good, trusting therapeutic relationship, we can really help. We can take time to support them to write a letter that they feel comfortable with, working therapeutically as we go.

Sophie's son Harry, had been adopted as a baby 11 years ago. The adopters had written faithfully every year and Sophie had been a bit hit-and-miss with her response: sometimes, with the help of the letterbox coordinator, writing back and sometimes not. She always found it a very difficult and painful process and never felt happy with what she had written.

I had come to know Sophie well. I helped her to find ways to respond to the things that the adopters had said about her son and to think about the things that her 12-year-old son might be interested to hear. I pointed out things that I knew about her like the fact that she liked to paint her bedroom in bright colours, reminding her of stories that she had told me (she was a great story teller!) like the time when a lost dog had followed her home and exploring with her what she had been interested in when she was 12 so that she could tell Harry. Harry had sung in a school production and she wrote that she too loved to sing but only in the privacy of her own home and that unlike Harry she would never have been brave enough to stand up in front of an audience! All the time I made sure that we used Sophie's own words: I might suggest something and then together we would dismantle my carefully constructed sentence and Sophie would say it out loud in her own way.

> Once we had completed her letter and read the final version through.
> Sophie said happily and with satisfaction, 'That is the first time in 11 years
> that I have written a letterbox letter that feels like it's from me!'

Necessarily, there are guidelines for writing letterbox letters and rules about what can and cannot be included. In order to best protect the children, birth parents are not allowed to say things like; they wish that the children were still with them, or that they believe that the decision to remove them was wrong, or that they long for the day when they will see them again. Of course, these are often *exactly* the kind of things that some birth mums or dads want to say. As a therapist working with a birth parent to write their letter, I try to provide them with a space to think, to feel and to say all of these things, to hear them and to process with them what it is like to not be allowed to write them. This then gives them the best chance of being able to reach a place in which they can construct a letter that meets the guidelines and allows them to say some of the other things that they want to say.

Writing a letter that will, perhaps just a week or two later, or if not at some point in the future, be read out loud to their child or read by the child herself, is often a labour of love. This is the closest that a birth parent will get to their son or daughter, a precious opportunity to communicate as mother to child or father to child and recognition that they still have a meaningful role in their child's life.

> Louise was very aware of the significance of this. She didn't want to type her
> letter but instead used an old fashioned ink pen, knowing that her children
> would touch the same paper that she had touched and feel the ink that had
> flowed from the pen that she had held.

> Harriet wasn't a confident writer but she went out and brought sticker books
> from the children's television programmes that the adopters had written that
> her son and daughter liked to watch. During our session she looked through
> the books and carefully selected stickers that she imagined they would like
> and then stuck them around the border of the writing paper.

Conclusion

The examples given in this chapter illustrate just how significant these opportunities for contact (whether face-to-face or via the written word) can be for birth mums and dads. Contact arrangements have understandably been developed to best meet the needs of the child and to give them the best chance of going on to live an emotionally heathy life.

But these moments of contact also have the potential to be either devastating or incredibly valuable and precious for the birth parents and to have an enduring impact on the lives that they live after the adoption of their child. An understanding of this and sensitivity from the professionals involved, can make a huge difference to people who are attempting to find ways to live with the painful loss of their children.

Part III

A Group Work Model (After Adoption)

Chapter 8

Breaking the Cycle: An Approach to Group Work with Birth Mothers

Daljit Gill and Bethany Lambert

This is not how my story will end.

Overview

Breaking the Cycle is a programme for birth mothers delivered in the Midlands by the independent adoption agency, After Adoption. Breaking the Cycle aims to provide intensive support to birth mothers, who have lost at least one child to adoption, in order to 'break the cycle' of repeated adoptions. Breaking the Cycle recruits birth mothers who demonstrate clear motivation, commitment and willingness to engage in the programme, which focuses on reflection and change. Participation is voluntary – birth mothers choose to take part in the programme.

Jess tentatively, but with a sense of pride, offers some seaside rock to the other group members, who accept with enthusiasm and interest in her recent holiday. Sue shows the group the clothes and new shoes she has bought for herself that morning with accompanying 'oohs' and 'aahs' from the others. She beams with pleasure. Enis chats happily with Daljit, talking about the new job she has just started. Christine joins the group slightly late and in a fluster. Bethany welcomes her with a smile which exudes warmth and acceptance, settles her in her seat and makes her a cup of coffee. The atmosphere is relaxed and informal. There is a sense of these women coming into this group and being known by others and in this process, coming to know themselves.

These birth mothers are coming close to the end of their journey on the Breaking the Cycle programme facilitated by After Adoption. In this chapter we will take you on a journey through Breaking the Cycle: first setting the scene by explaining the benefits of group work and the background to the programme, outlining the aims and approach and providing an overview of the content. At the end of the chapter we will also summarise the outcomes of this unique programme. There are two case studies which will give you an idea of the background and experiences of some of the birth parents, including a birth father, who have attended the programme. In this safe space these birth parents have found their voice to speak the unspeakable and to be heard. It is not easy listening to their experiences. Many were yesterday's neglected and abused children who were failed by the system. Some now hope to be tomorrow's parents.

The core elements of effective group work with birth mothers

At the heart of the Breaking the Cycle programme are our group sessions. The benefits of group work with birth parents and birth mothers in particular have been well documented (e.g. Jackson, 2000; Slettebø, 2011; Battle *et al.*, 2014). The types of group in these papers vary from structured, closed groups to more open-ended, unstructured groups. Overall these studies conclude that these group interventions had been helpful for birth parents.

Salveron, Lewig and Arney's (2009) review of the group work literature in this field identifies four common factors that help define a high-functioning group, these are: a non-judgemental environment, client participation, leader's stance of acceptance and relevant content.

The primary purpose of our group sessions is to provide an empathetic, non-judgemental space for birth mothers. Our approach is trauma-informed and strengths-based. To meet the complex and changing needs of the group workers have needed to be flexible in their practice. They have achieved this by 'Bending the Frame' (Eversole, 1997) to facilitate and maintain a connection and dialogue with group members in a respectful and non-judgemental manner.

Birth mothers have already completed one-to-one sessions with a worker prior to attending the group. This connection is a significant factor in engaging them with the group alongside meeting their practical needs (e.g. paying travel costs).

Workers have experience in group process and development and use this knowledge to manage the group dynamics and guide the group activities and discussions. Given the intense nature of the groups and the different learning styles of participants we use a range of delivery modes (e.g. group discussion, case studies, craft work and multi-sensory activities). Along with trauma, anger, shame, grief, isolation, stigma and trust are some of the key emotional themes that emerge throughout the life of each group. Workers are therefore continually assessing the learning needs and energy levels of the group in order to support the emotional regulation of group members.

Identifying the need

Parents whose children have been removed from their care often come from backgrounds of poverty, neglect and abuse and may have spent their own childhoods in care, or they may have experienced poor parenting. Our experiences of working with birth parents indicate that they are living on the margins of society: some have substance addictions, many are in poor housing, on benefits and have low levels of educational attainment. The trauma of the loss of their child can exacerbate existing problems and many attempt to replace the child with another, resulting in serial losses. Research has demonstrated that children who have been in care are almost 2.5 times more likely to become teenage parents compared with those brought up with both birth parents and looked-after children of both sexes are often more likely want a baby by the time they are 20 years old than young people living with their families (Corlyon and McGuire, 1999). Many perceive parenthood as an opportunity to compensate for their own negative experiences of family relationships and being parented. Anecdotal evidence from agencies suggests that these women may be repeating the cycle of becoming pregnant and losing the child to adoption because they crave the attention given by professionals when pregnant. This attention is a stark contrast to their 'typical' lives.

Background to the programme

After Adoption became aware of the high number of repeat adoptions that were occurring in the West Midlands: particularly those involving birth parents who were young care leavers. This region has areas of high unemployment and are some of the most economically deprived communities in the UK. These factors, coupled with the wish of Local Authorities to offer more effective support to birth parents, prompted After Adoption to choose the West Midlands as the location to develop Breaking the Cycle, their pilot support programme for birth mothers.

After Adoption secured external funding to deliver Breaking the Cycle twice a year from September 2014 to August 2016, with each cohort supporting five to seven birth mothers. Originally it was thought that the programme could support 12 participants in each cohort. However early on in the programme it was evident that these women had experienced complex trauma in their lives. Given the complexity of their needs, After Adoption decided to run the programme with fewer birth mothers in each cohort. This meant that participants could be better supported emotionally and encouraged to work towards their identified goals. Each birth mother that was referred was invited to take part in an assessment to explore whether the programme was suitable for them.

Approach and aims of the programme

The aim was to create a therapeutic programme which supports birth mothers to embark upon a personal journey of self-reflection, healing and repair. The programme aims to improve mental health and wellbeing, and encourage and inspire birth mothers to take control of their lives in order to make positive, informed decisions and choices in the future with an increased likelihood of entering rehabilitation, education, community activity or employment.

The focus of Breaking the Cycle is to help birth mothers address the issues underlying the loss of a child to adoption. It differs from other projects that offer similar services in that it encourages a journey of personal change and gives emotional and practical support to enable birth mothers to parent subsequent children. This is particularly important given that research undertaken by Lancaster University (Broadhurst *et al.*, 2017) indicates that 24 per cent of birth mothers subject to proceedings to have their children removed will repeat this experience within seven years. Breaking the cycle also supports birth mothers to make informed choices about contraception and future pregnancies. Unlike Pause, another service provided for women who have had children removed from their care, Breaking the Cycle does not stipulate a requirement for women to be using contraception to allow them access to the programme. Breaking the Cycle also does not exclude birth mothers who are pregnant at the point of referral.

Birth parents are often understandably wary, anxious and fearful of interventions facilitated by social care. An independent service is more likely to be able to engage this traditionally hard to reach group. After Adoption has a long history of providing counselling and intermediary services to birth parents on behalf of Local Authorities who recognise that a contracted-out independent service for birth parents does help to facilitate engagement.

Breaking the Cycle is also unique in offering a structured, therapeutic programme, which is flexible, bespoke and tailored to the needs of each birth mother. The staged structure of delivery, which first engages birth mothers in one-to-one sessions to build relationship and rapport, and then moves them on to group sessions, is very effective. This group are traditionally hard to engage yet birth mothers who attend this programme tend to complete it and engage in the follow-on drop-in sessions.

Content and structure

The content of Breaking the Cycle was developed from the practice knowledge and experience in After Adoption of working with a range of different service user groups, including teenage parents. It also draws on the breadth of experience and skills that exist within the agency in supporting birth parents and on ideas and materials from the well-established SafeBase Therapeutic Parenting programme. Breaking the Cycle draws on the strengths-based approach in SafeBase, which seeks to develop and strengthen the personal resources, confidence and resilience of parents and to develop the specific skills needed to care for and nurture a child based on therapeutic parenting techniques and strategies.

The programme is split into three sequential phases:

1. Six one-to-one sessions which support birth mothers to understand their life journey and the reasons associated with the removal of their child/ren from their care.

2. Six group work sessions focused on supporting birth mothers to: build self-esteem and confidence; understand the cycle of grief and loss; recognise the value of healthy relationships; understand the impact of stress and depression on emotional health and wellbeing and understand the importance of self-

care and nurturing. A key component of the group work is the opportunity for birth mothers to meet other mothers who have also lost a child/ren to adoption. This may be the first opportunity the birth mothers had to share their stories in a safe, supportive and non-judgemental environment.

3. A six-week optional parenting programme for birth mothers who are pregnant or want to have children in the future to gain a greater understanding of parenting. This element of the programme aims to provide birth mothers with an insight into 'good enough parenting', attachment and cycles of interaction, child development, early brain development and safeguarding.

In addition to these three phases, a monthly drop-in peer support group is available to all birth mothers who have completed the programme.

An important element within the structure of the programme the folders each birth mother compiles of the work they complete during Breaking the Cycle. Birth mothers talk about the value of assembling and writing down their experiences and how the process helped them to acknowledge their difficult experiences, reflect on their past and also plan for the future.

Quotes from birth mothers in the following sections are from the evaluation of the programme by Coram (quoted in Bellew & Peeran, 2017).

One-to-one sessions: 'You have to be the hope'

The focus of these sessions is to help birth mothers understand their life journey and the reasons why their children were removed from their care. The majority of birth mothers who access the programme have traumatic histories, feel hopeless, isolated, lonely and unsupported and have had limited opportunities to build meaningful and supportive relationships. It takes time for them to feel safe enough to talk honestly about their experiences and feelings. During the sessions their narratives are visually recorded by the worker in the form of a road map.

Childhood trauma and abuse, at their core, are about being and feeling unsafe. Creating a framework of physical, emotional and psychological safety is therefore vital to this process. In these sessions birth mothers are given the space to tell their story for the first time with respect and without judgement in a safe space. Other professionals may have heard pieces of their story but in our experience no one has listened to their whole narrative. The majority of birth mothers have never put their thoughts and feelings into words and been able to speak what has previously been unspeakable. Their stories are often filled with unexpressed raw pain and intense grief. In terms of a trauma-informed approach we know that putting feelings into words and constructing narratives of experiences helps emotional regulation and understanding and leads to the experience of a more coherent sense of self.

> When I done this, this is the bit that shocked me though. Because I didn't think I had been through that much things in my life.
>
> Anna (Bellew & Peeran, 2017, p.33)

> It took me years to get it out because I was having this anxiety, trapped, isolated, I had no foggiest idea where it was coming from and then when I found out doing the one-to-ones... I wonder how long I have been brewing all this up for; I wonder how long I would have been going on going through this. It made me realise now I can identify my body better now which is good...what a massive release.
>
> Theresa (Bellew & Peeran, 2017, p.20)

As part of this process workers are also helping birth mothers to understand the nature and impact of trauma on their sense of self, how they see the world and relationships and to be able to reflect on any maladaptive coping strategies that they have developed in order to survive.

> Before I just couldn't [make my own choices] because I just didn't know what to do. And, like, I was in care myself... Well, like, when you ain't been treated properly and you've been brought up...[in a] really poor upbringing, well how can you learn?... Because it affects you when you're growing up, when you're a child, see. It...affects you, mentally, up here. It affects you. And that's when, well, that's when things go wrong.
>
> Alice (Bellew & Peeran, 2017, p.23)

Creating and communicating a sense of hope in these sessions is also important. Whilst empathising with experiences of hurt, grief and despair the worker also holds onto visions of the birth mother's potential future self by identifying and building on their internal and external resources.

It became evident that the birth mothers enrolled on the programme had all experienced differing levels of complex trauma in their lives. As such, the one-to-one sessions were tailored to each birth mother's needs. Consequently, the timeframes in completing the individual sessions varied between six and 14 weeks, as opposed to the initial expectation of six sessions completed in six weeks. This has highlighted the importance of a bespoke programme that is needs-led and delivered at the right pace for each birth mother.

The nature and intensity of this work inevitably has an impact on workers. Access to clinical supervision and the space and time to debrief and reflect on sessions is essential.

> There have been times where we've listened to someone's story and we've been speechless...you can't get it out your head, you go home thinking about it...we talk to each other and offer support.

> I'm really experienced but there've been times during this that it's wrong on so many levels that someone has been through all this without the right support or help.

> (Bellew & Peeran, 2017, p.35)

Group work: 'Being seen'

Following completion of the one-to-one sessions, birth mothers are invited to join group sessions which are held weekly over a period of six weeks. It is a closed group that consists of four to six participants. These sessions focus on supporting birth mothers to: build self-esteem and confidence; understand the cycle of grief and loss; recognise the value of healthy relationships; understand the impact of stress and depression on emotional health and wellbeing; and understand the importance of self-care and nurturing. Travel is reimbursed, drinks and snacks are provided and the group members are asked what they would like for lunch. The sessions are held 11–3pm.

Building rapport and trust in a safe environment where group members feel accepted and valued is at the heart of the process. The atmosphere is relaxed and non-judgemental, which enables birth mothers to begin to engage with their peers and with the group process. The style is conversational, inviting and fun with lots of repetition. The facilitators work hard to create a nurturing and caring atmosphere by making the drinks, providing snacks and conveying empathy and understanding even when group members arrive late.

The content is inclusive and engaging and delivered at the right pace. Each session includes a range of visual and interactive activities, many of which are completed while participants are talking. This helps them to regulate as it is much easier to 'do' and talk. Creative activities include collage, mask making, mirror work, making cards with positive affirmations and writing an advert for a partner. Group members enjoy debating scenarios, for example about 'good enough' parenting and domestic abuse. This helps them to begin to discover their voice, think for themselves and have their point of view valued and to learn how to agree to disagree. A range of worksheets are used in the sessions that encourage self-reflection. Mindfulness is an important part of the group process: encouraging participants to notice what is happening in the here and now in terms of feelings, sights, sounds and taste. They particularly enjoy the chocolate tasting sessions!

During the course of the group sessions the group members create a 'virtual' birth mother who is given a name by the group. This figure provides a distancing tool which helps group members to share their painful feelings and experiences. It helps them to acknowledge and talk about the impact of trauma in their lives. This birth mother looks a complete wreck, has no mouth, is crying and self-medicates using alcohol and drugs; she has a broken heart that is full of emptiness, anger, sadness and fear. As the group progresses this virtual birth mother begins to change in her appearance. This reflects the gradual transformation of the individual group members as they engage in the process. The virtual birth mother is now looking after herself, her hair is now styled and she is wearing smart clothes, lipstick and nail varnish and has a big, wide smile.

Group members have the opportunity to make a memory box for their child in recognition that they are still the birth mother of their child. They are encouraged to hold their child in mind and to write letters and cards to them from the heart. This is often in stark contrast to how they are asked to phrase letters for their letterbox arrangements. The memory box also creates opportunities for them to talk about their child, for example what they may be doing now or what they might have bought them for their birthday or Christmas.

An important element of the group process is celebration of, for example, birthdays and achievements. Celebrations take place in the group and in between sessions group members are shown they are held in mind by the facilitators sending birthday and Christmas cards or messages with simple personalised affirmations. Birth mothers are also provided with a journal (in addition to their work folder) in which they can write or receive positive messages about themselves and can keep completed activities from the sessions.

Group members begin to realise that they share a common experience and begin to reach out to each other to offer support and understanding. Birth mothers talk about no longer feeling isolated and alone. They can feel and be supported and begin to make new friends.

> I've made a friend... Because she's been through similar, the same as me... You can learn from each other really. And like you can help each other. Like if you get stuck.
>
> Alice (Bellew & Peeran, 2017, p.30)

> It has helped me make new friends, because before I even started on this course I had none. I didn't even have one. Now I've got like three or four.
>
> Mel (Bellew & Peeran, 2017, p.30)

> Well we used to encourage each other didn't we? If like one of us was not understanding a certain module, or it was difficult for that person...we would break it down for each other, so like you would understand it.
>
> Katherine (Bellew & Peeran, 2017, p.28)

Managing the group process is challenging and requires a lot of energy. One worker observed: 'Sometimes I feel like I am a mum with six children pulling at the apron strings'. The workers are modelling respectful and healthy relationships and their interactions are often watched carefully by the group. The workers also act as parents to the group: managing the competition for attention until group members begin to have the confidence to talk to and support each other. Flexibility and sensitivity are also needed in managing the group. Often group members arrive late, get upset or leave early. Careful thought needs to be given to the language used and how concepts and issues are explained. Group discussions also need thoughtful and sensitive management. At the end of the session workers comment that they often feel that they 'have been hit by a bus'.

The group work sessions help birth mothers learn ways of identifying and understanding their needs and feelings, which helps them feel more in control of their lives and begin to feel more optimistic:

I've learned things I never even knew about myself and I can put into perspective now where I failed and where I didn't.

Claire (Bellew & Peeran, 2017, p.20)

Future parenting: 'Now we can look to the future'

There is a six-week optional parenting programme for birth mothers who want to have children in the future, gain a greater understanding of parenting or who are pregnant. This element of the programme aims to provide an insight into 'good enough' parenting, attachment, child development, early brain development and safeguarding.

A two-hour monthly drop-in peer support group is also available to all birth mothers who have completed the programme. This is an open group and on average five to seven birth mothers attend each session. There is plentiful tea and coffee and cake! The focus is on therapeutic activities that help to lower anxiety and stress (e.g. mindfulness). There is also the opportunity to revisit topics of interest identified by group members.

The group needs sensitive and thoughtful management as often birth mothers attend with a *'need to say it all'* and it would be easy for one individual to dominate a session. Group members are still learning how to manage relationships and can easily fall out with each other. The group gives opportunity for birth mothers to socialise and make and develop friendships and meet participants from other programmes.

Just going out, or if I was staying in I would just try to do things in [the house] I think some of the time, or most of the time, with my ex-partner, I had no choice half the time, because he were just locking me in and keeping me in. And now I just can't get enough of going out... I focus on things I can do, rather than things I can't do. Believe in myself.

Lara (Bellew & Peeran, 2017, p.26)

Outcomes: 'Finding our wings'

Breaking the Cycle had a positive impact on the birth mothers who participated in the programme. The programme was particularly successful in being able to maintain a high level of engagement from the birth mothers who all had complex histories and needs (birth mothers reported feelings of sadness, depression and anger before the programme). It was likely that the tailored and staged approach (beginning with one-to-one sessions and progressing to group work) contributed to this level of engagement and created a safe and open space for the birth mothers to reflect on their pasts and make positive steps towards their futures.

(Bellew & Peeran, 2017 p.7)

At the time of writing (August 2018), 43 birth parents have enrolled on Breaking the Cycle, 12 are currently coming to the end of the programme.

Of the 31 that have now completed Breaking the Cycle:

- One birth mother disengaged during one-to-one sessions.

- Four left the programme after completing the one-to-one sessions: one moved out of the area, one secured full-time employment, one enrolled into college and one relapsed into substance misuse.

- Twenty-six completed the programme.

- Ten chose to complete the optional parenting element.

The evaluation report of the pilot programme states that the programme 'achieved all of its intended aims' and highlighted some key areas.

Wellbeing

All of the birth mothers' wellbeing increased as a result of the programme. The birth mothers interviewed discussed how their self-esteem had improved as a result:

> ...still be hating myself, I'd still be upset... I'd be just unmotivated. I wouldn't want to see nobody... Because I've just, well, I've come to terms with it now and I'm just starting to build my life up again. Get my confidence back, get my self-esteem back and...going out more and doing things more, going out...with my partner.

Lara (Bellew & Peeran, 2017, p.19)

Five birth mothers went on to access counselling and therapy following completion of the programme.

Moving on and accepting

An important change for the birth mothers after Breaking the Cycle was the improved ability to accept the loss of their child.

> I think it has been the final nail lifted out of the coffin really. Because I had private therapy and was referred to mental health groups from the NHS. They were really good. But this was the final thing that made me really, you know, come out... Because in those other groups and with my therapist and that, I felt like I couldn't really talk about how I was feeling about my child and my feelings surrounding that. But in this group I could. Because everyone has gone through the same.
>
> Anna (Bellew & Peeran, 2017, p.34)

Positive life choices

The programme encouraged the birth mothers to make positive life choices, which included living healthier, being more active or seeking employment, education or training. The majority of birth mothers reported an improvement in this area after the one-to-one sessions. Birth mothers now felt able and more confident to engage in employment, education and other positive activities in their community.

- Seven birth mothers are now in employment.
- Four are actively engaged in voluntary work within their communities.
- Six birth mothers engaged with education through university, college and online courses.
- Two of these women completed an access to nursing course and have made applications to university.
- One has graduated from university.

Birth mothers have contributed to the continued development of After Adoption services: BirthTies, Families that Last, representation on the Breaking the Cycle advisory group and active participation in the Ofsted inspection which took place in 2017.

Relationships

Birth mothers on the programme had limited experiences of positive, supportive relationships in their lives. Birth mothers were able to develop trusting relationships with both professionals and their peers in the group. After the programme, birth mothers felt more comfortable talking to someone about their children. Consequently birth mothers felt much less isolated in their situation.

Parenting skills

Of the birth mothers who completed the programme six women are now parenting.

- One birth mother enrolled with a child on a child protection plan; she is now successfully parenting with no Local Authority involvement.

- Two birth mothers have had older children returned to their care.

- Three birth mothers who enrolled onto the programme whilst pregnant have their children in their care.

- Nine birth mothers who have children in permanency placements have reported improved quality of contact with their children.

One birth mother had won the right of appeal at Placement Order stage of adoption, had been rehabilitated with her son and was parenting him with Local Authority involvement.

One birth mother felt that Breaking the Cycle had made a very positive difference to how she managed reuniting with her 18-year-old son, including how she viewed his adoptive parents.

Conclusion

In reflecting on and developing Breaking the Cycle we have found that the combination of one-to-one sessions progressing to ongoing group work has been highly effective in supporting birth mothers. Our regular drop-in sessions allow birth mothers the opportunity to stay connected with their peers and professionals once they have finished the programme. Through telling the story of their loss and listening to the narratives of others, group members have found support and acceptance. Acknowledging and celebrating strengths has had a positive effect on their wellbeing and self-worth, which has enabled them to take more control over their lives. This has helped them make significant behavioural and lifestyle changes. Developing skills in emotional regulation and communication has also helped these birth mothers to find more helpful ways of managing interpersonal relationships and relating to professionals.

> It's more the fact of understanding that how you feel inside and all the things that you are going through, like the grief process, it was okay to feel like that and that it wasn't that you were going mental. Because you could speak to anyone else. It was the opening up and being able to relate to other people that was more important to it... Because sometimes you feel like you can deal with it. But once it has come out it has made me a stronger person. I thought 'Wow I can cope with this now'.
>
> Theresa (Bellew & Peeran, 2017, p.28)

References

Battle, C. *et al.* (2014) Groupwork for parents whose children are in care: challenges and opportunities. *Australian and New Zealand Journal of Family Therapy*, 35: 327–340.

Bellew, R. and Peeran, U. (2017) After Adoption's Breaking the Cycle programme: An evaluation of the two year pilot. September 2014 to August 2016. Coram. Retrieved 26 February 2019 from https://www.afteradoption.org.uk/wp-content/uploads/2017/01/Breaking-the-Cycle-final-report-Aug-2017.pdf

Broadhurst, K. *et al.* (2017) *Vulnerable Birth Mothers and Recurrent Care Proceedings.* Lancaster University and Centre for Child and Family Justice Research.

Corlyon, J. and McGuire, C. (1999) *Pregnancy and Parenthood: The Views and Experiences of Young People in Public Care.* London: National Children's Bureau.

Eversole, T. (1997) 'Psychotherapy and Counseling: Bending the Frame. In M. Winiarski (Ed.), *HIV Mental Health for the 21st Century.* New York: NYU Press.

Jackson, J. (2000) Developing a post-adoption group work service for non-consenting birth mothers. *Adoption and Fostering* 24(4): 32–39.

Salveron, M., Lewig, K. and Arney, F. (2009) Parenting groups for parents whose children are in care. *Child Abuse Review*, 18(4): 267–288.

Slettebø, T. (2013) Partnership with parents of children in care: A study of collective user participation in child protection services. *British Journal of Social Work* 43: 579–595.

Part IV

Creating Space for Change: Supporting Women Who Have Experienced Recurrent Care Proceedings (Pause)

Chapter 9

Taking a Pause: An Innovative Approach to Working with Women Who Have Experienced Multiple Removals of Children[1]

Sophie Humphreys and Ellen Marks

Still fighting when first met Pause.

Lost.

Broke down.

Time to rebuild.

Want to be a better me, something my kids can look
to and be proud of.

Lost a stone, bike rides, gym, getting healthy.

Smaller me, bigger confidence.

Gained the old me, before him.

I'm a winner.

I shine.

---

1   With thanks to Pause Practices, who have shared experiences and learning which have
contributed to this chapter.

Other chapters in this book explore various clinical and therapeutic models for working with birth parents whose children have been removed and placed for adoption. However, there are a group of women (and we suspect men) who do not take up these offers of support. What happens to them? This chapter explores an innovative new approach: Pause.

Pause works with women who have had, or are at risk of, repeat removals of children from their care. We aim to break this cycle and give vulnerable women the opportunity to develop new skills and responses that can help create a more positive future. We do this by working with women at a time when they have no children in their care and our ultimate goal is to help reduce the number of children going into care.

Having begun in Hackney in 2013 as a pilot, an emerging positive evidence base has supported the growth of Pause across multiple sites in England and, soon Scotland and Northern Ireland. Pause Practices are delivered by a variety of Local Authority and third sector partners, in collaboration with Pause.

This chapter sets out the need for Pause and its origins, written by Sophie Humphreys, Pause founder and chair. It then goes on to describe how model works, written by Ellen Marks, director of practice and learning. Both Sophie and Ellen have first-hand experience of this issue from their times as children and families social workers.

The case for Pause

Sophie Humphreys, founder and chair of the Board of Trustees

When I think back on my experience as a frontline practitioner – running the child protection service at the Homerton Hospital and in strategic and advisory roles in Hackney – I can remember the cases that drove my determination to develop an intervention for women who experienced repeat removals of children into care. With nothing changing, these destructive cycles would repeat year after year for the same women. When it came to developing the Pause model, one woman in particular has always stayed at the forefront of my mind.

Her name is Clara. When I first met her, Clara was 28 years old and had already had two children removed. She was pregnant again and initial proceedings were underway for her third child.

Clara had grown up in and out of foster care. Her father was physically abusive towards her and her mother was an alcoholic. During her time in foster care she was sexually abused by one of the carers and as a result Clara was understandably distrustful of services, particularly social workers. To Clara, the world was a hostile and dangerous place.

Clara found it very hard to contain her emotions when caring for her own children. She developed a complex personality, found herself in a catalogue of difficult relationships and was either the victim or perpetrator of domestic violence. The combination of unresolved emotions and angry outbursts was putting her own children at risk and resulted in their removal. Clara was a bright young woman, who at times was able to recognise the risk she posed to her own children, but could not regulate her emotions and behaviour.

Fast-forward 12 years, to when Pause was at last becoming a reality and I saw Clara in the street. She told me she had just had her ninth child removed. For Clara, the years between child number two and number nine were filled with chaotic relationships, compounded trauma and bereavement from the repeat losses she had experienced, painful feelings numbed through drug and alcohol abuse, unstable housing and, most pertinently, a lack of the right support. This meant Clara carried on giving birth in the hope she could fill the gap left after each pregnancy, both metaphorically and literally. Clara was in a battle with the Local Authority, the 'corporate parent' that had let her down as she herself grew up. She held steady to the need to 'keep one baby' and win this battle.

Sadly, Clara is not an exception. For anyone involved in the family justice system, it is not uncommon to meet women with similar stories. One will have seen dozens, if not hundreds, of cases brought before the judge, where a woman stands poised to lose her child for neither the first nor the last time. You know, too, that when they walk out of the courtroom, without an intense intervention being offered to help break this destructive cycle, there is too high a chance of them returning in the months or years to come. Perhaps, like me, you wondered if there was a better way of doing things that would result in better outcomes for these children and women. A way of 'doing things differently', by intervening and filling that gap with something different: something other than another baby, who will inevitably end up being removed and the subsequent grief and trauma that follows. A 'pause' was needed to create a space for change, and so, Pause was created.

In 2012 a feasibility study revealed that in Hackney alone, 49 women had given birth to 205 children who were taken into care[2] and this led to London Borough of Hackney agreeing to fund a Pause pilot.

These were many of the same women I had seen at the Homerton hospital, in courtrooms and out and about on the streets of Hackney over the course of my career. They felt like 'forgotten women'. We knew that this was not a problem confined to Hackney but experienced across the country. It is only recently that a comprehensive national data set has truly demonstrated the scale of the issue. This study estimates the scale and pattern of recurrent care proceedings over a seven-year period (Shaw *et al.*, 2014). The numbers are significant, showing that of a total of 46,094 birth mothers appearing before the courts, 15.5 per cent were linked to recurrent care applications. As each woman may be linked to more than one child, the total number of care applications associated with this cohort is as high as 29 per cent (22,790).[3]

The numbers of women are shocking, but we must also remember another number: that of the number of children being taken into care. The mission at the heart of the Pause approach is to prevent the damaging consequences of taking thousands more children into care every year. By working systemically through the lens of the woman, Pause helps them take control of their lives and break the destructive cycle that causes deep trauma both to them and their children.

The initial study not only exposed the numbers of women and children affected, it also gave us an insight into services. This was not just about the women learning new ways to navigate their world, but also the professionals who interact with them. There were many services and professionals who were doing their best to support women who were caught in this cycle, but they were all having to operate within the confines of their own organisational and professional systems.

For people who found 'typical engagement' patterns hard to maintain, offering appointments in clinics or only communicating by post was unlikely to hit the spot. As a result, good services with skilled professionals were wasting precious time and resources because women were unable, for one reason or another, to take up the support. This mismatch between service design and the needs of some of the most vulnerable people in our country meant not only was this cycle

---

2   S. Humphreys, G. Perry & L. Vanes: A report on the feasibility of establishing a pilot project aimed at breaking the cycle of birth mothers repeatedly giving birth to children who are subsequently removed, 2012.

3   see www.escholar.manchester.ac.uk/uk-ac-man-scw:227563

of children going into care being repeated, but valuable resources were being wasted by being out of step with need.

As part of the initial feasibility study we undertook a comprehensive cost–benefit analysis. The findings were startling – and when presented to the director of Children's Services and the Local Authority director of finance funding for the pilot was agreed in 2013. Georgina Perry and I co-designed the integrated model that underpinned the practice of the first Pause pilot.

The numbers were compelling and the need for successful intervention is clear. The early success and impact of the Hackney pilot drew attention from others and, thanks to successful bids to the Department for Education's Innovation Fund, Pause started to grow. At the time of writing, the 20th Pause practice has just opened and we have a central unit coordinating work and capturing evidence to inform and influence local and national policy, for both vulnerable children and adults.

The Relationship is the intervention: the Pause model in action

Ellen Marks, director of practice and learning for Pause

The Pause model works in partnership with Local Authorities where there is a Pause practice to identify potentially eligible women for the programme. These will be women who have had two or more children removed, are at risk of becoming pregnant and having that child removed into the care system. Our practitioners then work tenaciously and creatively to try and engage women, offering them a bespoke programme of practical and emotional support for up to 18 months. Taking this pause offers women the space they need to take control of their lives, finding new ways to overcome the problems of the past, meet the challenges of the present and build a better future.

Pause is about building relationships – relationships with women, relationships with other professionals and agencies, as well as relationships with their children and wider family members. If a woman has experienced harm and trauma in the context of a relationship – either as a child or as an adult – it is only through the context of a relationship that mastery and recovery begin to take place.

The Pause practitioner works towards developing a genuine relationship by spending time with the woman, presenting a different version of a professional relationship from what she may have experienced before. The practitioner tries to maintain a consistent presentation where they are predictable and overtly demonstrate that the woman is being held in mind. This lays the groundwork for challenge to be received and tolerated. This is a relationship in which the woman will be valued and respected for who she is as a woman, not simply in relation to her maternal identity or presenting issues – a relationship where a woman is encouraged to discover or uncover her individual identity, needs and aspirations. This is different to the negative perspectives and language that many women will be used to hearing about themselves. We focus on achieving what, from the outside, might seem small steps that offer a sense of value and worth, but we know are giant strides forward for the women themselves.

We are often told that some women are 'difficult to engage' or 'hard to reach'. Undoubtedly women we work with may be living complex and chaotic lives and they will have experienced many professionals in their lives, often with negative outcomes. Women have often built up hostility and mistrust towards services or agencies that have worked with them. Public law care proceedings are adversarial and complicated. Women tell us time and time again that they didn't understand the process, nor did they always realise the significance of what they had done, or not done, until it was too late.

Women are also accustomed to being told what to do and why they need to make changes by professionals. But change is hard for everyone, no matter what it is. Talk to anyone who has tried to lose weight or stop smoking or do more exercise and you'll hear lots of accounts of why things haven't worked. The women we work with are no different from you or me in this regard, tempting as it might be to see them as being 'other'. For the most part they have simply not had the good fortune to experience childhoods that helped them mature into adults who can successfully navigate the complicated social world in which we live, as they have not been provided with the foundations needed. For many, the abuse and trauma they have experienced has hindered aspects of their development. Few Pause participants have come through this with the coping skills or problem-solving ability to navigate life successfully. Many have high adverse childhood experience (ACE) scores and the evidence shows that these will have an impact in later life in a multitude of different ways.

In response, women develop coping strategies which may aid survival in the short term, but, longer term, can become maladaptive and cause harm, both to the women themselves, to their sense of worth and self-esteem and also to those around them, including their children. It is this that makes the work of Pause so complex. Women have likely been victims of childhood abuse, of domestic violence and coercive relationships. Alongside this, their own actions and/or behaviour have also caused harm to their children. This is more often by omission than by commission, but it is harm nevertheless. The guilt and shame, as well as anger, loss and grief, make for a very complicated environment for Pause practitioners to operate within.

In the development of the Pause programme we made a deliberate decision not to follow a manualised approach. Manualised programmes have many strengths, but too often lives don't follow their required structures and we want to enable innovative practice, not stifle it. Instead we have a framework that is designed to ensure fidelity and integrity to what matters but allows flexibility to encourage local ownership and adaptability. This means ensuring that we recruit not only a highly skilled workforce, but also individuals whose values and beliefs are compatible with the Pause core principles. This gives us professional trust in Pause people and, in turn, allows them to work with a degree of autonomy that respects their professional expertise. With this comes responsibility and accountability. We recruit practices from wide professional's background including statutory social care, health, criminal justice, housing and third sector. Practitioners are encouraged to be creative and solution-focused, drawing upon a range of established theories and delivering evidence-informed interventions, tailored to the individual women. These include, but are not limited to:

- attachment theory
- trauma-informed practice
- social learning theory and role modelling
- systemic practice
- strengths-based approaches
- motivational interviewing
- cognitive behavioural therapy
- mindfulness and mentalisation
- social prescription.

In an assertive outreach model, we do not send appointment letters, carry clipboards and forms or invite women into the office for assessment; instead we take the work into the community where they are. Pause practitioners seek out the women that Local Authorities have identified as being eligible for Pause, make contact with them, explain the service and what it offers. This takes time, creativity and tenacity as women are rarely where we expect them to be.

Too many systems fail to recognise the reality of the lives vulnerable women lead and the impact it has on accessing and communicating with professionals. If a woman is living in a tent, in the corner of multi-storey car park, how do you send her an appointment letter? When women are sent an 'opt-in' letter from mental health services and do not respond or attend they are recorded as 'did not attend' (DNA) and are then discharged from the service. She may be at the address, but too depressed or guilty and ashamed by what has happened in her life to make use of the services she is being signposted to. How many people can follow signs at these points in their lives? Or she could be homeless or sofa-surfing and never got the letter, but she is sitting in front of us outside the supermarket or coffee shop begging for money. And this is where Pause suggests the work should begin – by sitting down next to her and beginning to talk as one human being to another, with compassion.

We expect many women to be unsure about whether they want to take up the offer of Pause. While some do welcome it immediately, asking why it's taken so long to be asked, many are uncertain. They are surprised that anyone is interested in them now that they no longer have children in their care. They tell us that they are not worth our attention and they are surprised if we come back after they have sworn at us and told us to go away. Therefore, we have built an extended 'engagement phase' into the 18-month programme, giving women four months to decide if they want to take up the Pause offer.

During this time we also explore their thoughts and feelings about contraception. Pause is a programme for women who want to take a break in childbearing – and the most reliable way to do that is to use contraception. Having in place a reliable form of contraception is a condition of moving to the next phase of the programme and we support women to access local sexual health services to ensure they have the best advice to meet their needs. If, after the initial four-month period, women aren't ready to take a break from pregnancy, we don't believe our programme would be right for them and will help them find other, more appropriate services.

For many, Pause comes into their life at a time of crisis and chaos. This is not the case for all but it is common to meet women who are homeless, without benefits and without access to medical treatment other than attending A&E. When we first meet a woman, if she needs and wants help, it is provided, there and then, regardless of whether she has formally agreed to 'sign up' to Pause. These early stages of engagement are about demonstrating through our actions that we will do what we say will do. They also indicate that we are interested in finding out about a woman, getting to know her and showing her that we are dependable. We also show that we will keep coming come back, over a long period and that we can tolerate and sustain the relationship through the inevitable ruptures and repairs that we know will follow.

Rita had five children removed from her care and found it very hard to trust anyone. There was ongoing chaos in her life, linked to substance misuse (crack use) and sex work. Just to meet her required exceptional determination from her Pause practitioner. She did not give up and over a period of two years she called into the homeless hostel where Rita lived and reminded the staff there that Pause was still hopeful for this woman. Sometimes Rita would agree to meet, only to then disappear again. At other times she wouldn't turn up at all.

She was finally moved to another hostel and this led to her asking the staff there to contact the Pause practitioner who had been looking for her for so long. They have now met more regularly and Rita has decided she wants to work with Pause, so they are seeing each other in a more frequent way, though there are still aspects of her life which are chaotic.

Through this work Rita has been updated about her youngest child, who has been adopted. With her practitioner she sat in a local park reading letters from the adopters, something which Rita has previously been unable to face.

It seems unlikely that without the two-year history of being looked for and being thought about, with the practitioner demonstrating that she was holding Rita in mind, Rita would have sought out this help.

When a woman agrees that she wants to sign up for Pause she is agreeing to up to 18 months of individualised support. Practitioners deliver individual bespoke interventions to meet a woman's practical and emotional needs, following the model in Figure 9.1.

Figure 9.1: The Pause model

While there is a therapeutic aspect to all of the work, we do not describe the work as therapy. It does not have the structure or formal boundaries of clinical treatment and recognises that, at this stage in their lives, the women require something different. If the women we work with were living stable enough lives that allowed them to come to counselling or therapy on a regular weekly basis, or were in a position to be able to recognise and talk about their feelings, it's likely that they would not have found themselves in the situations that they are in.

What we have found is needed is intensive practical support to help stabilise, an interested and reliable person with whom to experience a non-abusive relationship, and time and space to stop, think and hope for the future – whatever that may be – for herself as woman. For most of the women we work with, this stabilising work needs to take place before any type of formal therapy or counselling can be accessed in a meaningful way. The basics of life need to be in place.

All of the work with the Pause practitioners has therapeutic underpinnings. It always involves talking, reflecting, thinking and being curious with women, with the practitioner taking on a dynamic and, if needed, motivating and challenging role. It rarely takes place in the confines of a professional setting or a room with two people sitting opposite each other. Instead it takes place out in the community, in homes or hostels, while going for a walk or a bike ride, or on the bus, over a cup of coffee or while waiting for an appointment. It takes place in face-to-face conversations and (when women have access) over the phone, via text, email, Snapchat or WhatsApp.

We know that many of the women we work with need longer term specialist clinical treatment. However, if the woman herself does not agree with this, or is not even able to acknowledge that there is a problem, or is so chaotic that we can't find her, then all referrals to specialist services are likely to go nowhere. This just reinforces the professionals' belief that 'she won't engage'.

Equally, although women often have complex issues, they do not always meet the strict threshold or diagnostic referral criteria for services and can therefore slip through the net of current provision once they are no longer responsible for a child. Whilst every parent whose child may be placed for adoption is entitled to specialist birth parent counselling, the experience of women on Pause is that this provision varies hugely. Many women are often not aware of this entitlement and even when they are they may not be able to practically or emotionally to access it.

We believe it is far better to provide women with the support in a way that they can access and in a way that feels safe for them. In time, this may allow her to develop a level of insight and sense of agency in acknowledging and accepting the need for specialist services in the future. There is far more likelihood of references to specialist services being taken up when the person themselves agrees – this may be for birth parent counselling, drug and alcohol services, DV services or mental health input.

What we have found is more effective is an altogether more dynamic and active intervention which combines practical and emotional support in a high-level way, seeing women at least weekly and, at times, daily if needed.

Along with this high level of support comes a high level of challenge, but one in which a woman's expertise in her own life is championed. Practitioners do not position themselves as experts, but neither are they women's friends. They offer a different experience of a professional in which they are not there to rescue or direct women to a particular pathway. No one likes to be told that they need to make changes in their lives – even if it seems obvious to others that it is needed. So, we don't tell women they have to make changes, to leave violent relationships or to end substance misuse – even though we may strongly want them to – instead taking a harm reduction approach.

We use creative methods with women – craft activities, cooking and baking, walks in the park or on the beach, learning to ride a bike, yoga sessions or singing in a choir – which all provide experiential social learning opportunities. Women start off with intensive one-to-one work and, in time, there are group activities for those who want to join in. For many this is the first time that they have met other women who share their unique experiences of loss and it can be affirming to realise that you are not alone and the feelings that you have are not abnormal. For women who have poor dental care linked to drug use, self-neglect or abuse, having the courage to turn up and have a cup of tea in front of others can be a huge challenge for some.

But group work can also be complex. As well as bringing together women with a range of complex personalities, it is not unusual for there to be a sort of hierarchy between the women depending on their situation – 'your kids got adopted, but mine are on an SGO', which is perceived to signify differing degrees of harm caused to their children. Managing this, both in the moment and the aftermath, takes skill and confidence.

The activities, whether in a one-to-one or in a group setting, often bring a sense of fun to women's lives and accomplishment if trying something new. This should not be dismissed as we all need an element of fun and enjoyment in our lives. They can also help develop skills of concentration and problem solving. However, it is the reduction of social isolation and the reflective conversations that take place around the activities that bring most value – spending time together, talking about what is working for them and what is not going so well.

Practitioners use these times to explore ambivalence, to come to understand what is most important to the women and also to discuss what the possible consequences might be of the choices they make. In this way our practitioners take on the role of 'agents of change', working systemically with women wherever they are.

The women's lives, both personal and professional, do not exist in silos. They are members of families, friendship networks and communities, and we need to work with all of these systems. When working with partner agencies we encourage them to think differently by working with the women from an open and curious perspective, putting aside any previous preconceptions and assessments. On a case-by-case basis, practitioners challenge and advocate for women. This might be explaining to a Local Authority why we do not think it fair to expect her to walk 16 miles to collect the travel warrant she needs to enable her to attend the final contact with her child, or liaising with the local drug service to explain that she was half an hour late as she was at the DVT (deep vein thrombosis) clinic and she should still be seen and given her prescription. On a wider strategic level these issues are taken up in local areas to ask partner agencies to think about how they run contact services, letterbox services, housing provision for vulnerable women, and access to GP and dental services.

What systemic working means to us is that if a practitioner is working with a woman who is staying with a family member and that family member is being sanctioned by the Department for Work and Pensions and, as a result, they have had had no electricity for 10 days then, with their consent, they will make some calls and support the family member to try to resolve the problem. Or if a woman is in a relationship with someone who is themselves struggling with substance misuse and has expressed some interest in exploring treatment options, we would help set up an appointment and, if they wanted it, we would accompany them to their initial meeting. The woman remains the focus, but we do not ignore those around her, or the impact they may have on the woman.

What have we learnt?

That it takes time – you cannot do this work with high caseloads, so our practitioners work with a maximum of eight women. This low number may be perceived as a luxury but working in such an intense way brings other complexities and challenges – it is incredibly complicated and demanding. All practitioners have access to clinical supervision, which is essential for this highly intensive work with complex and vulnerable women. Our recruitment process is thorough, as is the induction process and there is an on-going programme of learning and development events offered to all Pause practitioners.

We have learnt that we must have a healthy relationship with risk: many of the women live in highly risky situations and we can mitigate but not remove this. We have to make 'risk sensible' decisions and be able to tolerate, both individually and organisationally, the anxiety this brings.

Viewed through the lens of Pause participants, we are learning that we professionals do not make contact with children easy enough. Contact will always be extremely complicated for a whole range of reasons. We ask adoptive parents or foster carers to support a process with adults who have caused harm to their children and we ask birth parents to acknowledge that their children have other families, other mums and other dads. We then ask children to move between these two worlds, often written into care plans in a very formulaic way, e.g. letterbox contact twice a year or face-to-face contact six times a year. Contact should always put the needs of the child first and those needs are likely to change throughout their life. We know that there are times when contact is absolutely not in a child's best interest, but we also know that when a birth parent is able to take part in contact and to do so consistently and reliably, then this will have benefit for the child and their sense of belonging. For many, this can be a stabilising factor and contribute to better long-term outcomes.

Karen was only 19 when she was approached by her local Pause practice. She has had two children removed from her care. Although she was never formally 'looked after' herself, she had lived in 15 different places between the ages of 14 and 19 as her family life broke down and she sofa-surfed. She continues to have a very volatile relationship with her family.

Pause met Karen at the end of the final hearing for her second child and she later told us: 'I always say no to professionals and I did with Pause. But they turned up when they said they would at court. I never thought they would do that.' Being different in her eyes allowed the practitioner to begin to build a relationship which Karen was open to.

From this the practitioner was able to support her in a number of ways, including to attend a meeting with the adopters of her second child. Planning and preparation work took place, together thinking about what she would like to know, helping her identify and write down questions and checking with the child's social worker if these questions were appropriate. This prevented any disappointment for Karen as she was prepared and able to ask the questions that meant the most to her.

She was able to take part in the meeting, which was incredibly difficult for her. As a result of the courage she has shown, she now has pictures in her mind of who will be raising her child and had an opportunity to know who they are. Equally the adopters can say to their child, 'yes we met your birth mum, she looked like this...'

We've also learnt that outcomes for women vary significantly, but all are celebrated. Some women's lives are still very complicated at the end of the 18-month programme: some look very different, others less so. This is as we expected. Some women lose regular contact with their Pause practitioner for weeks or months, but we don't give up on them and most resurface eventually. For some women to have a relationship with another person in which you are held in mind, in which they want nothing from you, in which you are valued just for being you is the only 'goal' of the 18 months. Others are able to make significant changes in their lives, uncovering talents and skills and resourcefulness they didn't know they had.

Dawn had been working with Pause for three months, after having seven children removed from her care. She was keen to work with Pause and welcomed the intervention, seemingly coming at the 'right time' in her life. Early Support had already helped move her to stable housing. Further interventions were focusing on relationships, alcohol issues and offending behaviour.

She had never worked but was desperate to buy her children Christmas presents with her own money and set a goal of getting a job. However, feelings of anxiety and fear dominated her attempts to find work. Her coping mechanism with this, and life in general, was alcohol, although she was not a dependent drinker. She would drink to calm herself, drink to excess and arrive at interviews intoxicated. When she didn't get the job this reinforced the vicious circle of inadequacy and sense of failure.

Her practitioner used their time together reflecting and being curious as to what might be behind the drinking, rather than trying to problem solve. They saw each other regularly, often several times a week and over time they were able to begin to unpick patterns and link them to feelings. Dawn began with small steps to putting in place other coping strategies.

With her practitioner's support she was able to find out about local agencies who placed people in factories for work trials without needing a formal interview. This seemed a good option for her and they did lots of preparation, planning and role playing together to help her prepare and she got a trial. However, despite feeling ready, unsurprisingly on the first day she was crippled by anxiety and fear - but, because they had done lots of planning, rather than drinking she called her practitioner and asked her to 'call in sick' for her.

They talked at some length with the practitioner both supporting and challenging her. She helped normalise the feelings, using mentalisation techniques again to talk about 'racing hearts, feeling sick and/or being sweaty'. Her practitioner explained that the feelings she was having were felt by pretty much everyone in these situations. Their relationship was strong enough that she could challenge Dawn and suggest that if she put it off until the next day the chances were that her feelings would still be there. In talking it through, Dawn was able identify that, despite having thought she could do it, being alone and going to something new was too frightening for her. So together she and her practitioner agreed that she wouldn't have to do this alone. Her practitioner picked her up and took her to the factory, going in with her to the security desk to begin the shift. She also arranged to be available for a phone call during breaks if Dawn needed someone to talk with to help manage further anxiety during the day. Once supported to get there and with the back-up plan of a phone call, Dawn was able to carry on with her first day.

Being with her, planning and preparing, being alongside her, sharing the anxiety and encouraging her was what Dawn needed to be able to walk through the gate. Several months on she is still working and is no longer on the agency crew. She has been taken on by the factory full-time and is working a regular 40-hour week. Not only does this give her financial independence but also a sense of pride, of worthiness and of being 'normal', which is helping transform her life.

Sadly, we are also learning from women that they have come not to expect compassion from services. Pause has now worked with over 400 vulnerable women with all the complications, complexity and joy that this brings. Our challenge to other services is that it is not right to say that there is a section of society that will not engage. As professionals we have to work smarter, we have to take responsibility and find ways to reach out to communities that are marginalised, traumatised and frightened. Undoubtedly there are differences between Pause as a voluntary programme and statutory services, both children's and adult services. We recognise that we come into women's lives at a different point and our focus is different. We do not have all the answers, but we believe that there are aspects of our approach that could be of benefit to mainstream services when working with vulnerable populations.

Pause matters to me because it's given me time to take a look at my life as me, not as a mother, not as a daughter, not as a friend - as me and what strengths I have and what I need to improve on. To get back to the person I was before I had troubles in my life.

I have a better understanding how my mental health affected my parenting. I can now ask for help easier than isolating myself. It has also helped me see things from my children's views and feelings better.

Reference

Shaw, M. *et al.* (2014). Recurrent care proceedings: Part 1: Progress in research and practice since the family justice council 6th annual debate. *Family Law*, 44(9), 1284–1287.

Conclusion

Karen Treisman

This book offers an important contribution to the literature base around supporting and further understanding and advocating for birth families in the context of adoption. This provides a spotlight and expands on the crucial area of birth families within the wider world of child protection, adoption, fostering, care proceedings, relational trauma and beyond. This book also sheds some light on and powerfully presents some of the multi-layered complexities which birth families face throughout their lives following the removal of a child/children. Each chapter covered different elements and angles, however, there were several common and overlapping themes and key points which I will aim to present in this conclusion, before going on to summarise some of recommendations which the contributors have shared for further supporting and understanding birth parents.

First, each chapter brought the complex and, at times, unique needs of birth families to the forefront. This book not only aims to promote greater insight and compassion for birth parents and the multiple and diverse challenges which they can face, but also is a crucial contribution given that they are often a neglected, punished, blamed, stigmatised and unsupported group of people. Some of the complex needs highlighted in this book which the authors feel need to be considered when thinking about the experience of birth families include the following (not an exhaustive or prescriptive list):

- Birth families experience a loss which is visceral and body-based. Nancy Verrier talks of this experience as being a primal wound – and how these losses can be encoded in one's sensory and body world. Carole Green powerfully described this loss and void in her chapter as the hole that is left. In addition, birth families also experience a trauma and a loss, unlike bereavement, which is often misunderstood, which is less common and where the grief is often disenfranchised and socially invalidated.

- Birth families also often have to live with and face the shame, judgement and blame which can surround being a birth parent/relative where a child/ren has been removed. This can be received or perceived from relatives, services, friends, societal discourses, media and from one's self (e.g. internalised stigma).

- Birth families need to navigate the complexities of the court system and legal processes which in themselves can be a maze and at times an oppressive and traumatic experience. Let alone when birth families are also at the same time, often in survival mode, in shock, having to fight, having to make sense of what has happened and so forth.

- Birth relatives also need to contend with the painful and overwhelming processes and tasks which often follow court. Including for example, having to say goodbye, write later life letters, contribute to life story work, negotiate and manage possible ongoing contact and cope with the crushed hope of being reunited with their children. This is often in the context of limited support and often also having to do this when they actively disagree with the decisions which have been made.

- Birth families often have to respond and cope with frequent reminders and triggers of their child/ren, of parenting and of the insurmountable losses which they are facing and continue to face. For example, doctors asking about their medical history, children's birthdays/festivities, seeing child and pregnancy reminders everywhere, and people regularly asking if they have children, or where their children are.

- In addition to the above, birth families also can experience the pain which can be associated with having future children. For example, watching their other children progress and develop well can cause some of the losses and associated feelings to resurface, such as guilt. This can also occur when, for example, a parent has been using drugs and then has managed to stop using drugs leading to feelings of guilt, regret, but also of wishing they could turn back the clock and perhaps anger, as to why they couldn't have made these changes earlier.

- Birth families also need to contend with fears and uncertainty about what will happen to their children, what sort of life they will lead, where will they live, who will look after them. What will their children know and be told about them. What will happen to important elements of their children's identity, such as their name, their religion and their traditions. This can be even more difficult when birth families disagree with the choice of adopter/carer, and/or when their children have been placed separately and, therefore, are not with their brothers or sisters.

- As captured throughout the book, the vast majority of birth parents have experienced their own trauma and adversity during childhood and often throughout their lives. Thus, for many birth parents they may experience feelings during the process of removal, such as, 'I am not good enough', 'I am worthless', 'I am a failure' and 'I am not important', which can sadly echo, mirror and resurface how they may have felt about themselves as children (and throughout their lives). Therefore, this can add weight and pain to these powerful thoughts about themselves (core beliefs, internal working model, early schemas/scripts), assumptions and emotional hotspots. In addition, birth relatives may feel powerless, helpless and hopeless within the decision-making process, which again can mirror and echo how many people feel during trauma and maltreatment – powerless, trapped, silenced, helpless and so forth. This can unfortunately then reinforce, layer and embed these beliefs even further, causing further pain, and subsequent survival and coping responses.

- We know from statistics that removals are more common for those families who themselves have been in the care system and/or are recent care leavers. Therefore, having a child going into the care system may mirror the parent's own care history. In many cases, this may be associated with negative feelings and memories. Often birth parents have described to me during court assessment and therapy that this was their biggest fear. This can also contribute to feelings of fear, guilt, rage, shock, regret, sadness, unfairness and injustice.

- As captured throughout the chapters, birth parents understandably often feel wronged, misunderstood, attacked and hurt by services/professionals/authority figures. They also often have a strong sense of unfairness and injustice. Therefore, this can understandably significantly impact their relationship to help, support, authority and to systems which means that trust, opening-up and relinquishing control can feel like a mammoth and at times impossible and counterinitiative task. This can show itself in engagement difficulties and extreme caution, but also can feed into the increased sense of isolation which birth families can often feel and which is evident throughout many of the poems and vignettes in this book: Who do I turn to, who will help me? Who has my back? Who cares?

- For birth families, often the coping and survival mechanisms which were some of the reasons why children were removed in the first place may be exacerbated, or new ones may arise, following the physical and legal removal of the children. So, we may see an increase in risk. For example, using drugs or alcohol, difficulties emotionally regulating, dissociating, self-harming, feeling low, being in risky relationships, self-neglect, criminal behaviour, getting pregnant again and so on. Carole Green in Chapter 3 talks of some of these behaviours as ways women are trying to fill a hole, a void. This echoes the work of people such as Gabor Mate, who advocates that instead of asking people why the addiction we should be curious and asking why the pain. This loss and trauma-based behaviours are also exacerbated further, as many women describe their children as their main protective factor and reason to live and, therefore, once a child is removed, this can not only increase the presenting risks, but also can remove a key protective factor from them. This was captured in a woman whom I worked with recently sharing, 'What do I have to live for? What is the point? The only thing I cared about is gone.'

- Birth relatives also need to take on the hugely complex and ongoing task of trying to make sense and process what happened and why it happened (often with little to no support), whilst also having to mourn the losses (which often haven't been named). But they also need to renegotiate a new identity: 'Who am I? Am I a parent? Why am I here? What will I do? What does my future hold? What is next?'

- Birth relatives may also be contending, as captured by Pause and in other chapters, with numerous practical difficulties which also may be exacerbated by the removal of their children, which can have financial and housing implications.

The above complexities and unique considerations are particularly valuable, given that as demonstrated throughout this book, birth families are often under-supported, neglected and can easily fall through the net and under the service radars. This is due to an interplay of factors which were discussed throughout, ranging from the primary focus and priority of the system being placed on the children, to difficulties with services having the resources, skill and strategy to engage with birth families, to birth families often being blamed and shamed, through to birth families often being a denigrated, marginalised and stigmatised group. The neglected needs of birth families are also reflected in the scarcity of suitable, tailored, long-term, flexible and matched services and resources for these families. Birth families are often left with little to no support, or support which is not adequately tailored to their needs, or to short-term conditional interventions.

To give further weight to the need for the development, support and investment of these sorts of services, this book encapsulates some of the individual, family, systemic and societal benefits of proactively supporting birth families through the huge losses and traumas which they experience. Some of the advantages and benefits of developing, supporting and improving these types of services and resources for birth families include:

- It is essential to intervene proactively and preventatively with birth families, in order to not only support them as people and as fellow humans, but also to try to influence the cycle which often occurs, of women having repeated removals of children, or women unfortunately engaging in further unsafe behaviours. This has social, psychological, physical and financial short- and long-term implications. This intervention and support to birth families is also crucial given the overwhelming evidence we now have available to us around epigenetics, family scripts, intergenerational transmission of trauma and the generational and multi-layered impact of adverse childhood, cultural, community and adult experiences. Programmes like Pause, Adoptionplus and Breaking the Cycle group provide us with some proactive, tailored and innovative ways of contributing to this cycle change.

- As previously described, the majority of birth families have experienced significant amounts of relational and developmental trauma in their own childhoods and throughout their adult lives. They are often the children who the system was trying to protect, who have grown up. Or sometimes those who the system was not able to identify or protect. Therefore, like the children, they need and deserve support and interventions to support them around these traumas and adverse life experiences. For example, we know that trauma can affect people's bodies (including their nervous, immune and arousal systems), their brains, their self-concept, their tendency to dissociate, their relationships and relational styles, and their ability to regulate their emotions and their behaviours. In addition complex and cumulative trauma often impact on one's multi-faceted development, which can have a variety of consequences, including that people can respond in a way that is socially, emotionally and developmentally younger than their chronological age (Treisman, 2016). So, it makes sense that we need to not only extend the lens through which we look at children who have experienced trauma to their parents and take a life-span and generational perspective but also, to try to create services which meet parents where they are at socially, developmentally and emotionally, and for them to have access to trauma-specific and trauma-adapted interventions which also integrate knowledge around the unique needs of birth parents, including the multiple losses which they would have faced at having a child removed.

- Birth families are also likely to have further contact (direct or indirect) with their children; so, their own emotional wellbeing, behaviours, narratives and circumstances are likely to have an ongoing impact on their children, including on their identity and on the children's adoption experience.

- The system has made a decision to remove the child and, therefore, it is also arguably the system's responsibility and duty to support the consequences of that decision.

Therefore, with the above rationale for the increase in provision and quality of support for birth parents in mind, this book advocates for the need for more of these carefully designed services and for birth relatives to be viewed as a crucial part of the child protection process. This also posits that designated services not only take a trauma, loss, relational and attachment lens, but that they also are delivered in an empathetic, compassionate, non-judgemental and accepting way. This book also advocates for services (like Pause and Adoptionplus) to be more flexible, proactive and creative. This is in order to most effectively support both the long-term needs of birth parents, and to accommodate for the complexities which they may present with. After all, complex difficulties require complex solutions and approaches. These services should also ideally be shaped, developed and contributed to by those with lived experiences.

This book also suggests that services need to allow, or at least expect that there may be a dip-in and dip-out nature of engagement and that services also need to proactively meet the families where they are at and allow for services to be accessed and offered throughout their journeys, rather than as a one-off attempt at engagement. Research and practice experience has shown that the uptake of services and the level of engagement is far higher when services are offered throughout different time points of birth families' journeys. In the Introduction Joanne Alper also discussed how services can enhance their accessibility and engagement through being thoughtful and communicating the ethos, flavour and style of the service through contact methods, such as letters and phone calls, which also reflect the compassionate, sensitive and nurturing approach. Drawing on the various chapters, some other recommendations for the types of services needed follow:

- Services need to prioritise trust and safety. These are key components in both the engagement and intervention process, and are the bedrock of any relational and trauma-informed approach. These components are even more crucial given that many of the birth families would have understandably developed or most likely already had a complex and tricky relationship to help, power, support and authority figures reinforced. Therefore, the policies and service provision need to allow and support this relational flexible and longer term approach. Joanne Alper and Patricia Downing put this beautifully in Chapter 4 by saying we need to 'Open doors and build bridges'.

- Services also ideally, should be inclusive of all birth relatives, including birth fathers, who are often even more neglected within the overall process. Ian Orr-Campbell discussed some of the unique needs of birth fathers and also shared how birth fathers often present with more expressed aggression and anger (Chapter 5). However, Ian posited how it is about staying connected with the hurt underneath and working proactively with these men that is the reparative part. This also means it is even more important to support and truly listen to their voice, as they often feel othered, forgotten, judged and unimportant. This also fits with the notion that we need to see the behaviour as communication and to try to see the whole and the hurt person behind the behaviour, defences, the crisis and the situation (Treisman, 2016).

- As said previously, services need to try to model by being empathetic, compassionate, supportive, nurturing and so forth. This needs to be embedded and infused throughout every sphere of the service. People need to be treated in the way that you want to teach them to treat others. This is because birth parents need an experience which they can internalise, connect with and hopefully transfer and take forward. They need to have a different way of doing relationships and being in relationships (Treisman, 2016). They need to have an experiential experience, a felt experience, of what this is and what these can be. For example, if we want to support birth families to go on to be empathetic, nurturing, attuned, thoughtful, how we expect them to further develop and strengthen these skills, if we are not modelling and giving them an experience of it – for example, by keeping them in mind, by validating their experiences, by being compassionate with them (Treisman, 2016).

- Within the service, birth families need to feel listened to, heard and validated. This is so crucial given that in the process so many of them would have felt misrepresented, misunderstood, not listened to, silenced and ignored. This can echo the powerlessness, helplessness and hopelessness which is often associated with past traumas. Services unintentionally can echo this by being trauma-inducing and adding to this re-traumatisation. Therefore, to reduce this, services needs to actively find ways to be trauma-reducing and trauma-aware, and for there to be roles and opportunities for voice, collaboration, partnership, agency, mastery and choice.

- Building on the above, some chapters spoke about the power of group work and of having opportunities to connect with others and to have a role of supporting and joining with others. This format seemed to give some women a feeling of being part of a community, of being understood, accepted and to have a sense of belonging. Lizette Nolte and colleagues (Chapter 2) also captured this in one of their themes as, 'having someone in my corner'. This sense of belonging and community feels even more integral given the social stigma which some women can face, as well as the loneliness and isolation which can often be associated with trauma and loss.

- Some of the chapters, such as Chapter 9 on the Pause project, indicate that there are some important practical aspects which many women need support with and that this also has the advantage of improving parent–professional relationships and engagement. For example, around housing, tidying up, making appointments, practising what to respond when someone asks about whether they have children and so forth. This practical focus is helpful as it can give the families a tangible example and experience of being listened to, supported and seeing visible results. This can also make some physical and emotional space to move on to the more intensive therapeutic support, like that offered by services like Adoptionplus. This fits with Maslow's hierarchy of need theory. This also highlights the potential benefit of marrying services up, between those like Pause who offer this type of practical intensive support and those like that at Adoptionplus who offer a longer term therapeutic support.

- Several of the chapters discussed what a huge impact having a child removed can have on one's identity and on one's sense of self. Therefore, having time to mourn the loss and also re-connect and transition to a different life and identity feels like an important process of any intervention. This also means re-connecting with the person's other parts of their identity and personality and seeing them as a whole person, rather than by being defined by this one aspect. This also includes supporting birth families to begin when they are ready to integrate, process and engage in meaning-make around what happened and why (this is likely to include past traumas and adversity). It is also likely that families are going to need, in addition to the sense and meaning-making, some skill development and coping tools to support their emotional regulation and response to triggers.

- Several of the practitioners discussed the benefit of creative outlets and expressions. This is highlighted further through the powerful and moving poems which are peppered throughout this book and through some of the activities described by the work of Pause and the Breaking the Cycle group. For example, Breaking the Cycle discussed creating an externalised mother – 'A virtual mother' – who is then transformed so that the group members can visually see her journey and progress. This draws on creative tools, but also uses externalising and distancing tools as seen in therapies such as Narrative Therapy and Gestalt Therapy. These holistic interventions are key as trauma is a whole-body, whole-brain, multi-sensory experience and therefore it needs whole-body, whole-brain and multi-sensory approaches (Treisman, 2017).

- Similarly, many of the authors spoke about the importance of holding and sharing hope for the children, for the families and for all of their futures. This holding and conveying of hope feels like an integral part of the work and of any intervention. This should include interventions and services also having a focus around magnifying, celebrating, noticing and enriching birth families' strengths, resiliencies, protective factors and positive qualities.

- Lastly, there needs to be thought, careful planning and sensitivity around endings and goodbyes. Given that the nature of the work is about traumatic endings and goodbyes (with their children), the way this ending is done can be reparative and healing, or re-triggering and re-traumatizing (and all of the shades in between). Therefore, this needs attention and care.

With all the above in mind, there was also a clear recommendation for services to acknowledge the emotional, physical and spiritual toll that this type of work can have on the staff providing the services, and therefore the supervision, wellbeing and self-care needs of the practitioners need to be prioritised and actively supported. This includes, as Joanne Alper highlighted, that the services offered ideally need to be within a wider caring, compassionate, safe, secure, nurturing, trauma- and attachment-informed workforce culture. The workers themselves need to feel in safe hands, thinking minds and regulating bodies in order to be able to offer this space and feeling to the parents (Treisman, 2016).

My hope would also be that the take home messages and increased awareness from this book, alongside the powerful stories and poems from the women themselves, will not only offer a more compassionate perspective of the needs of birth families, but also offer a strong case for further high-quality and flexible support for birth families across the country, and guidance on some ways of doing and enhancing this. However, in addition, that the messages will also be shared through proactive campaigns, training and initiatives to try to educate and skill-up services and professionals (e.g. police, judges, lawyers, Independent reviewing officers, social workers, GPs etc.). this is even more important given how neglected, under-resourced, stigmatised and denigrated birth families are. Within this, there is also a dearth of literature within this area and it feels integral that more evaluation and research is needed, including that led by and for birth families, around the unique needs of birth families, the services needed to effectively and most suitably meet their needs, the optimal models and approaches for service delivery and around the interventions offered. There also should be more research about sub-groups within this population, such as teenage parents who have their children removed, those with a care history and those from particular cultural backgrounds.

It feels so important that as a society we make sure that we are supporting the whole family and not just one part; that we are creating a wraparound team around the whole family; and that we are working to interrupt cycles, change trajectories, and support growth and development. We need to try to see and connect with the person behind the behaviour and the situation, and to support and not add to the hurt and to more holes in their hearts.

References

Treisman, K. (2016) *Working with Relational and Developmental Trauma in Children and Adolescents*. London: Routledge.

Treisman, K. (2017) *A Therapeutic Treasure Box for Working with Children and Adolescents with Developmental Trauma: Creative Techniques and Activities*. London: Jessica Kingsley Publishers.

Contributors

Joanne Alper

Joanne Alper is a Director and Co-Founder of Adoptionplus, a pioneering therapeutic adoption agency. She is a qualified social worker and therapist, who has a background in local authority childcare. Joanne is a Trustee on the CVAA Board and has sat as a specialist adviser on the NICE committee for Quality Standards in Attachment. She has a strong interest in promoting and sharing research and evaluation that improves understanding and benefits children and families. Joanne has had eight books published, and is a passionate advocate for effective relationship based practice.

Patricia Downing

Patricia Downing is an Integrative Psychotherapist and mindfulness practitioner. She has an MA in Integrative Psychotherapy and Counselling, and has been accredited with BACP since 2009. Her therapy work has included birth relatives affected by adoption, and a wide range of client presentations, within various services. Patricia has also been facilitating eight-week mindfulness courses for adoptive parents over the last five years and has completed the three-part EMDR training.

Caoimhe Forbes

Caoimhe Forbes is an Assistant Psychologist and Psychological Wellbeing Practitioner working within the NHS. She has had over five years' experience working within a variety of settings ranging from high secure mental health to children and adolescent mental health services.

She enjoys working from a systemic model which enables her, where possible, to include family and carers in an individual's recovery. Her research to date has been driven by qualitative methods which aim to gain insight into the difficulties faced by minority groups within society, which in turn attempts to ensure they feel empowered and that their voices can be heard.

Daljit Gill

Daljit Gill is a social worker and was team manager for the After Adoption 'Breaking the Cycle' programme. Daljit has 30 years' work experience in local government, working with children and families in education and social care, as a nursery nurse, social worker and manager.

Kim S. Golding

Kim S. Golding, BSc, MSc, D. Clin. Psy. AFBPsS, is a clinical psychologist specialising in helping children in care or adopted from care. She is a DDP consultant and trainer, and is a board member of the DDPI as well as a director of DDP Connects UK. Kim is the author of several books and programmes written for parents, educational staff and practitioners supporting children with the experience of developmental trauma.

Jane Gould

Jane Gould holds a Postgraduate Diploma in Person-Centred Psychotherapy and Counselling and became BACP Accredited in 2011. Jane is also trained in DDP (level 1 & 2) and has worked as a birth relative counsellor for six years. She also works in private practice as a Psychotherapist and Clinical Supervisor predominantly in the field of trauma.

Carole Green

Carole Green is an accredited member of the BACP. She completed a Postgraduate Diploma in Counselling in 2005, and has undertaken additional training in Gestalt, Psychodynamic and Person-Centred modalities. She also holds an Advanced Diploma in Couples Counselling. Carole trained in post adoption counselling in 2008 and since then has completed further adoption related training, including

DDP Level 1 and Theraplay Level 1. She has a wealth of experience of counselling people affected by adoption, having worked in this field for over ten years. During this time, she has worked with birth relatives, adult adoptees, adopters and families. Carole is interested in the ways in which our bodies hold our past experiences and is working with this in her practice and has trained in Sensorimotor Psychotherapy Level 1 (Trauma) and Level II (Attachment).

Sophie Humphreys

Sophie Humphreys OBE is the Founder of Pause. She is a highly experienced independent advisor on child protection and safeguarding, providing expertise to central government and Local Authorities across the country. Sophie was appointed by Ministers to look at child sexual exploitation in Oxfordshire and is working as an advisor to the Royal Borough of Greenwich in developing a new programme to reduce risk to children through domestic violence (SafeCore). Sophie currently sits on the Ministerial Female Offenders Advisory Board and the Oxfam GB Independent Safeguarding Review Panel. She is also a member of the Cafcass board. Sophie was appointed an OBE in the 2019 New Year Honours list for services to children's social care.

Bethany Lambert

Bethany Lambert joined After Adoption with a Postgraduate Social Work Masters, having qualified with distinction. She initially worked with adopted teenagers in the 'TalkAdoption' project, then progressed her career by moving into the 'Breaking the Cycle' team. Challenging and inspiring, Bethany relished the opportunity to support the participating birth mothers to reflect, rediscover self and flourish.

Ellen Marks

Ellen Marks is Director of Practice & Learning at Pause, where she is responsible for the support of over 20 practices across England, Northern Ireland and Scotland and the delivery of the organisation's monitoring, evaluation and learning strategy. She has 25 years' experience of working with children and families in statutory, voluntary and CAMHS settings. She has extensive experience of managing services for looked after children, frontline child protection and families involved in court proceedings and is a former Principal Social Worker for an inner London borough.

Hannah Morgan

Dr Hannah Morgan is a Clinical Psychologist with considerable clinical experience working with looked after children and their wider networks. Her current clinical role in the NHS involves providing consultations to social workers and working together with professional and parental systems to promote functioning networks around looked after children and young people. She likes to work integratively, prioritising therapeutic relationships and drawing on systemic and psychodynamic understandings of families. She is interested in research which empowers groups of people who could be considered vulnerable and/or may be otherwise silenced in society.

Lizette Nolte

Dr Lizette Nolte is a Principle lecturer on the Doctorate in Clinical Psychology Programme at the University of Hertfordshire. She holds a Professional Doctorate in Systemic Psychotherapy and has practiced in the NHS and other health care settings for over 30 years. Her research interests relate to families living in challenging circumstances, particularly where parents experience mental health concerns, and areas where people are marginalised or excluded, with a commitment to equality and social inclusion.

Ian Orr-Campbell

Ian Orr-Campbell is an integrative accredited counsellor, clinical supervisor and mindfulness practitioner. He is accredited with the BACP and has been qualified since 1999. Ian has undertaken additional training in DDP (level 1 & 2), Theraplay (level 1 & 2), Sensory Attachment Integration, MBC Mindfulness and Nurturing Parent Mindfulness. He also obtained his training in clinical supervision at the Gestalt Centre, London. Ian has worked therapeutically since 2003 with birth parents who have had children adopted and is the clinical supervisor for the Adoptionplus Birth Relative Counselling Service. Additionally, he facilitates mindfulness programmes for foster carers, kinship carers, adopters and social workers and provides group supervision to a children's counselling service.

Karen Treisman

Dr Karen Treisman is a Highly Specialist Clinical Psychologist who has worked in the National Health System and children's services for several years. Karen has also worked cross-culturally in both Africa and Asia with groups ranging from former child soldiers to survivors of the Rwandan Genocide. In addition to holding a doctorate in Clinical psychology, Karen has undergone a range of specialist training courses including EMDR, Narrative Therapy, Dyadic Developmental Psychotherapy, Video Interaction Guidance, Sensory Approaches, and Theraplay. Karen is an external consultant, trainer, speaker, and assessor to a variety of Local Authorities and organisations and is also an expert witness and regularly undergoes a variety of assessments for court. Karen regularly attends and presents at local, national, and international trauma, parenting, and attachment conferences. Karen is also a TEDx speaker on the power of relationships and viewing behaviour as communication. Karen is the author of seven books and two sets of cards around trauma, attachment, and direct-working tools. Additionally, Karen is also a reviewer for the Journal of Adoption and Fostering.

Hannah Wright

Dr Hannah Wright is a Specialist Clinical Psychologist working in Greenwich Child and Adolescent Mental Health Service (CAMHS) with children and families where there are child protection concerns or where children cannot live with their birth parents. She is interested in research that creates change and makes a useful difference for people who are disadvantaged in society. Her recent research has aimed to improve the quality and accessibility of services to support looked after children, birth relatives and carers.

Subject Index

Author Index